Getting Closer to Japan
Living in Japan

Living in Japan

Andy D. Para

ASK Co.,Ltd.
Tokyo, Japan

Getting Closer to Japan
Living in Japan

Book design by   Masami Jimbo
Illustrations by   Hiroko Kobayashi
Editing by   Charles T. Whipple, Hiroko Kageyama, and Masako Iijima
Supervised by   Prof. Kaoru Kobayashi (Sanno University)
DTP and printing by   SHINANO CO., LTD.
ISBN 4-87217-064-4
Living in Japan

The information included is available as of February 2001.
The publisher cannot be responsible for any subsequent changes in said infomation.
First edition, March 2001

Printed in Japan

Contents

Foreword

The first step

One time after an extended stay in Japan, I went back home for a stay and somehow got into a discussion with a fellow American about Japan. He seemed quite disappointed to learn that there are no samurai, no ninja, and very few geisha girls walking the streets. But Japan is actually much more interesting than what he had imagined.

If you're just getting off the plane, get ready to experience a long list of firsts. Your first Japanese house, your first rush-hour train, your first Japanese room, your first bowl of fermented beans, your first day of grocery shopping, your first Japanese bath, your first sumo match. The list is endless. And while some things you will choose to experience over and over, other things you will think once is enough.

A year after I first arrived in Japan, I knew everything there was to know. I could have answered all your questions with great detail. But now I know very little about Japan, and what you may think is a basic question will leave me with a puzzled look on my face. Japan is so Western and so Japanese, so traditional and so modern, so advanced and so backwards. This makes it a very difficult country to understand and describe — an enigma within an enigma.

Having lived in Japan for some 15 years, I'm often asked for advice by newcomers about how to survive and enjoy their stay. Perhaps the best advice I can give is to try to experience Japan without trying to describe it. So instead of trying to help you understand Japan through words, this book will simply give you enough information to take your first step towards experiencing Japan.

Andy D. Para
February, 2001
Tokyo, Japan

Hiragana/Katakana/Rōmaji

あ	い	う	え	お
ア	イ	ウ	エ	オ
a	i	u	e	o
か	き	く	け	こ
カ	キ	ク	ケ	コ
ka	ki	ku	ke	ko
さ	し	す	せ	そ
サ	シ	ス	セ	ソ
sa	shi	su	se	so
た	ち	つ	て	と
タ	チ	ツ	テ	ト
ta	chi	tsu	te	to
な	に	ぬ	ね	の
ナ	ニ	ヌ	ネ	ノ
na	ni	nu	ne	no
は	ひ	ふ	へ	ほ
ハ	ヒ	フ	ヘ	ホ
ha	hi	fu	he	ho
ま	み	む	め	も
マ	ミ	ム	メ	モ
ma	mi	mu	me	mo
や	(い)	ゆ	(え)	よ
ヤ	(イ)	ユ	(エ)	ヨ
ya	(i)	yu	(e)	yo
ら	り	る	れ	ろ
ラ	リ	ル	レ	ロ
ra	ri	ru	re	ro
わ	(い)	(う)	(え)	を
ワ	(イ)	(ウ)	(エ)	ヲ
wa	(i)	(u)	(e)	o
ん				
ン				
n				

が	ぎ	ぐ	げ	ご
ガ	ギ	グ	ゲ	ゴ
ga	gi	gu	ge	go
ざ	じ	ず	ぜ	ぞ
ザ	ジ	ズ	ゼ	ゾ
za	ji	zu	ze	zo
だ	ぢ	づ	で	ど
ダ	ヂ	ヅ	デ	ド
da	ji	zu	de	do
ば	び	ぶ	べ	ぼ
バ	ビ	ブ	ベ	ボ
ba	bi	bu	be	bo
ぱ	ぴ	ぷ	ぺ	ぽ
パ	ピ	プ	ペ	ポ
pa	pi	pu	pe	po

きゃ	きゅ	きょ	りゃ	りゅ	りょ
キャ	キュ	キョ	リャ	リュ	リョ
kya	kyu	kyo	rya	ryu	ryo
しゃ	しゅ	しょ	ぎゃ	ぎゅ	ぎょ
シャ	シュ	ショ	ギャ	ギュ	ギョ
sha	shu	sho	gya	gyu	gyo
ちゃ	ちゅ	ちょ	じゃ	じゅ	じょ
チャ	チュ	チョ	ジャ	ジュ	ジョ
cha	chu	cho	ja	ju	jo
にゃ	にゅ	にょ	びゃ	びゅ	びょ
ニャ	ニュ	ニョ	ビャ	ビュ	ビョ
nya	nyu	nyo	bya	byu	byo
ひゃ	ひゅ	ひょ	ぴゃ	ぴゅ	ぴょ
ヒャ	ヒュ	ヒョ	ピャ	ピュ	ピョ
hya	hyu	hyo	pya	pyu	pyo
みゃ	みゅ	みょ			
ミャ	ミュ	ミョ			
mya	myu	myo			

General Information

[日本のプロフィール] *nihon no profīru*

Profile of Japan

❶ Hokkaido ❷ Aomori ❸ Iwate ❹ Miyagi ❺ Akita
❻ Yamagata ❼ Fukushima ❽ Tochigi ❾ Gumma
❿ Ibaraki ⓫ Saitama ⓬ Tokyo
⓭ Kanagawa ⓮ Chiba ⓯ Niigata
⓰ Nagano ⓱Yamanashi ⓲ Shizuoka
⓳ Aichi ⓴ Gifu ㉑ Mie ㉒ Toyama
㉓ Ishikawa ㉔ Fukui ㉕ Shiga
㉖ Kyoto ㉗ Osaka ㉘ Nara
㉙ Wakayama ㉚ Hyogo ㉛ Tottori
㉜ Okayama ㉝ Shimane ㉞ Hiroshima
㉟ Yamaguchi ㊱ Ehime ㊲ Kagawa
㊳ Tokushima ㊴ Kochi ㊵ Fukuoka
㊶ Saga ㊷ Nagasaki ㊸ Oita
㊹ Kumamoto ㊺ Miyazaki
㊻ Kagoshima ㊼ Okinawa

北海道
Hokkaidō

Sea of Japan

東北
Tōhoku

甲信越
Kōshin'etsu

中国
Chūgoku

北陸
Hokuriku

九州
Kyūshū

Pacific Ocean

関東
Kantō

四国
Shikoku

関西
Kansai

東海
Tōkai

Pacific Ocean

Japan or *Nippon*?

Japan is the only English name for Japan, but *Nihon* and *Nippon*, both written as 日本, are used in the Japanese language.

When Europeans started dealing with China, they heard about the country called *Rìběn* (sounds like [jih-pen]), in Chinese. The Europeans started saying Jipang (Japan) so that is how Japan got its English name.

Area and geography

Japan takes up 377,835 square kilometers of the planet, that includes 3,091 square kilometers of water. And a 27,751km coastline is rather amazing when you consider that the coastline of Australia is only a little longer at 33,535 km, and even more amazing when you think that more than 20 Japans could fit inside one Australia.

The country is not mountainous compared to the Alps or the Rocky Mountains, but it's certainly hilly. Tokyo, on the same latitude as San Francisco, is quite flat, but old paintings show that it too once had plenty of ups and downs.

Mt. Fuji

The highest point in Japan is the summit of Mt. Fuji at 3,776 meters (12,389 feet). According to legend, Fuji arose during a single night in 286 B.C. Geologically the mountain is much older than the legend asserts. The most recent recorded eruption of Fuji lasted from November 24, 1707 until January 22, 1708.

Mt. Fuji tops the list of things Japanese in the minds of the Japanese, along with cherry blossoms and kimonos. It's one of the most photographed and painted mountains in the world. Regarded as sacred by many, Mt. Fuji is visited annually by thousands of pilgrims from all parts of the country, and its slopes are dotted with numerous shrines and temples.

Prefectures

Japan consists of 47 prefectures. In the Japanese language, they are called *ken* (県), but there are four exceptions: Osaka-*fu*, Kyoto-*fu*, Tokyo-*to*, and Hokkaido. The prefectures are grouped into regions, with Hokkaido a region on its own.

Population

As of October 2000, Japan's population was estimated at 126,686,000.

Tokyo has a population of 11,837,000. Japanese make up 99.4 percent of the population. Non-Japanese, mostly Koreans, account for the remaining 0.6 percent.

Life expectancy

Japanese have the world's longest life expectancies at birth (1995):

	Females	Males
Japan	**82.83**	**76.39**
USA	80.1	73.4
France	81.84	73.92

(source : demographic yearbook 1996)

Religion

It's hard to decide if the Japanese are the most religious or least religious people in the world. There are an estimated 102,214,000 Shintoists, 91,584,000 Buddhists, and 3,169,000 Christians. These figures, along with shrines for worshiping ancestors in their homes, festivals, and religion-based marriages and funerals, would make you think most Japanese are religious. Yet wide-spread religious apathy also makes you think the opposite.

(source<http://jin.jcic.or.jp/access/religion>)

Language

The Tokyo dialect is considered Standard Japanese, and it's spread throughout the country by radio and television. There remains various accents, with *Kansai-ben* of the Kansai District (including Osaka, Kyoto and Kobe) and *Tohoku-ben* of the Tohoku District are most well-known.

Weather and Climate

The Japanese love their seasons. You can see it in their poetry (*haiku*, 17-syllable poems, require at least one *season word*), in their letters (any good letter includes a reference to the weather), in their business suits (the switch from winter suit to summer suit days and back is synchronized with the seasons), and in their language (there are many words to describe the four seasons).

Whenever the Japanese list the seasons, they start with spring.

Spring (March, April, May)

Spring can be summed up in one word — *sakura* (桜) or cherry blossoms. Nationwide news programs announce the northward-moving "cherry blossom front" as the country warms from end of March to end of April. When it reaches your town, you take ground cloths, drinks, food, and friends to the park and make merry under the cherry blossoms.

It becomes chilly and cloudy during the cherry blossom season, called *hanagumori* (花曇り), but May brings fine, warm days.

Summer (June, July, August)

Here's the weather forecast for almost every day in June and July — rain. The season is referred to as *baiu* or *tsuyu* (梅雨). You think it will never stop.

When it does stop, be ready for the heat. From the end of July through August, temperatures range between 30 and 35℃ — hot. But add nearly 100 percent humidity and it feels like you're swimming in soup. A lot of the major festivals are in the summer evenings when the heat is much more bearable. Women frequently wear casual *yukata* kimono in the evenings and businessmen get to take off their suit coats. *Zansho* (残暑) is a word describing the heat of late summer.

Fall
(September, October, November)

The weather is usually at its best in the fall, with the exception of a few typhoons in September. Blue fall skies, referred to as *akibare* (秋晴れ) make October a great time to travel around Japan to take in all the fall harvest festivals.

The first snow in Hokkaido and the first snow on top of Mt. Fuji — beginning of October — are reported as national events.

Winter
(December, January, February)

The spring, fall, and summer seasons are quite similar throughout Japan — a little cooler in the north and a little hotter in the south. But winter is a different story. Northern winds blow in from Siberia bringing heavy snow and blizzards on the Sea of Japan coast. In Hokkaido, you'd think you were in Alaska, with four meters of snow (about 13 feet). But in Okinawa in the south, you may only need a sweater.

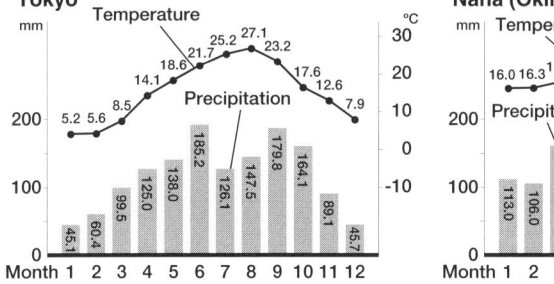

Monthly Mean Temperature and Precipitation (1961-1990)

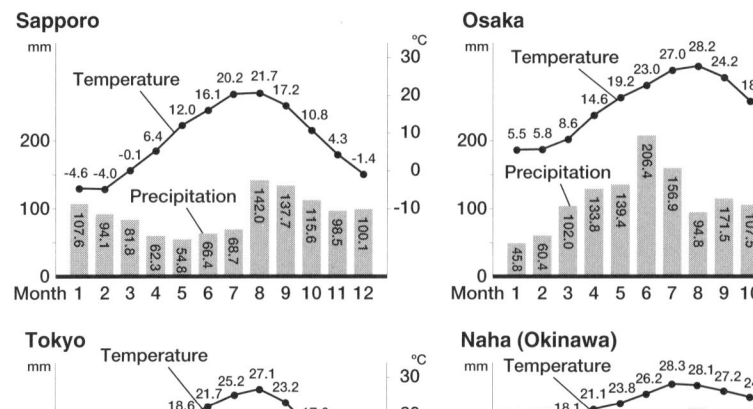

● Chronological Scientific Tables" 2000 「理科年表」2000

Japanese Holidays

●New Year (January 1-3) — *Shōgatsu*

The only official holiday is January 1, but most companies take seven to ten days off. *Yoi otoshi o* ("Have a good year.") is the greeting used several days before January 1, and *Akemashite omedetō gozaimasu* ("Congratulations on the opening of the new year.") is used when you meet someone for the first time after January 1.

A majority of the population on New Year's eve stays home and watches *kōhaku-uta-gassen* (The Red and White Song Contest), a TV show where male and female singers are pitted against each other.

Some stay up until midnight to hear the temple bells ring 108 times, but it's also traditional to wake up for the first sunrise of the new year. The post office delivers New Year's postcards (*nenga-jō*), usually designed with that year's animal from the Chinese zodiac calendar.

●Coming-of-Age Day (2nd Monday of January) — *Seijin no hi*

Cities often hold gatherings in auditoriums where new adults (people who have turned 20 in the previous year or who will turn 20 by April 1st) will dress up and go listen to speeches about being responsible adults. This is usually followed by wild drinking parties.

●National Foundation Day (February 11) — *Kenkoku kinembi*

According to ancient history books, February 11 in 660 B.C. was when the first Japanese emperor was crowned. This day passes with little fanfare, like an extra Saturday.

●Vernal Equinox Day (March 20 or 21) — *Shumbun no hi*

This national holiday is the time of the year for visiting graves.

●Golden Week (April 29 to May 5)

During this week there are four national holidays. Hordes of people take the week off and travel — which means it's a good time to stay home.

- Greenery Day (April 29) — *Midori no hi* (Golden Week)

It used to be celebrated as the birthday of Emperor Showa (the father of the current emperor). But since his death, it has been continued in honor of his interest in Japan's flora.

- Constitution Memorial Day (May 3) — *Kempo kinembi* (Golden Week)

Day for the new constitution that was adopted after the World War II.

▬ Between Day (May 4) — *Kokumin no kyūjitsu* (Golden Week)

A recently created national holiday to make the Golden Week continuous holidays.

▬ Children's Day (May 5) — *Kodomo no hi* (Golden Week)

Also called Boys' Festival. Traditional decorations for this day — and all of golden week — include carp-shaped windsocks, called *koi-nobori*, warrior dolls, called *musha-ningyō*, and replica swords.

●Marine Day (July 20) — *Umi no hi*

A very new national holiday — a good day to go to the ocean or to just stay home and have a good time.

●Bon Festival or *obon* (around August 13 - 15)

Obon is a Buddhist-oriental festival to commemorate deceased ancestors. This is not an official holiday, but most companies and government offices take this period off, resulting in congested roads and airports.

●Respect-for-the-Aged Day (September 15) — *Keirō no hi*

Respect for the elderly and longevity is celebrated on this national holiday.

●Autumnal Equinox Day (September 23 or 24) — *Shūbun no hi*

The week (*ohigan*) of the Equinox Day is the another time of the year for visiting family graves.

●Health and Sports Day (2nd Monday of October) — *Taiiku no hi*

This day in 1964 was when the Olympic games of Tokyo commenced, a day for sports and health-related events throughout the country.

●Culture Day (November 3) — *Bunka no hi*

A day for promotion of culture and the love for freedom and peace. On the culture day, schools and the government give awards for special, cultural activities.

●Labor Thanksgiving Day (November 23) — *Kinrō kansha no hi*

A national holiday to honor workers.

●The Emperor's Birthday (December 23) — *Tennō Tanjōbi*

The current emperor was born on this day, making it a national holiday. Whenever the emperor changes, the national holiday changes to the birthdate of the new emperor.

(When a holiday falls on a Sunday, the following Monday becomes a holiday.)

Daily Life in Japan

[日本で家を探す] *nihon de ie o sagasu*

Setting Up House in Japan

Going house shopping

If you have been transferred to Japan, your company will probably prepare your housing for you or introduce you to a real estate agent who can speak English. The system in Japan is probably quite a bit different from where you come from, so it's good to know what to expect. If you're apartment hunting on your own, getting a Japanese friend to go along will be a big help.

Major differences

Perhaps the biggest difference is that apartments are not rented directly from the owner, but through real estate companies. This gives you a wide variety of choices, but you also have to pay the agent a fee. In addition to the first month's rent, be prepared to fork over the following:

Binder (*tetsukekin*): Usually one month's rent to show that you're serious. With the binder in hand, the real estate agent will keep it for you. This money will be used for the deposit, but if you cancel out, you probably won't get it back.

Deposit (*shikikin* or *hoshōkin*): Two or three months' rent goes to the owner.

When you move out, this will be used to make repairs and cover outstanding rent. You'll get back anything left over, but don't expect much.

Key money (*reikin* or *kenrikin*): One or two months' rent as a "gift" to the owner — it's gone for good.

Agency fee (*chūkai tesūryō*): Maximum one month, by law.

Maintenance fee (*kanrihi*): For apartments, there can also be a monthly maintenance fee that covers such communal things as outside lamps, elevators, and janitor services.

Renter's insurance (*hoken*): Most places require you to pay the first year of renter's insurance, usually around 10,000 yen.

Japanese and non-Japanese alike need a guarantor (*hoshōnin*), who is liable for the rent if the renter defaults. Most real estate agents will require a Japanese person with indications of some social standing and money. Sometimes you have to show a bank passbook.

On your own

The rents in Tokyo are high. If you're looking for an apartment on your own, first decide where you want to live and then the terms and accommodations you want. Go to a real estate office, the Internet, or one of the English periodicals.

If you don't mind an hour and a half one way commute, you'll find rent much more reasonable. But if convenience is what you're looking for, be prepared to pay for it. While many Japanese live close to the city center when they're young, they'll often buy a house in the suburbs when they get married and have children.

Real estate offices

Not many real estate agents speak English. So you'll have much better luck if you can take someone with you to interpret. If you can narrow down your choice to a few apartments, the agent is usually happy to let you in to have a look. But be warned that some agents and owners have a no-foreigner policy.

English periodicals

Most of the English newspapers, magazines, and free papers have information on apartments. In addition to classified ads, there are companies that specialize in helping non-Japanese find places to live. Although the costs are much more expensive, they certainly save time and grief in finding what you want.

G o o d *to* k n o w

Internet for-rent ad

Mejiro   2 bedrooms Apartment   ¥ 600,000

Maintenance fee :	Include 2 months	Structure :	Reinforced concrete
Deposit :	4 months	Built :	March, 1999
Key money :	1 month	Facilities :	Heating and cooling, elevator, gas oven,
Location :	Shimo-ochiai, Shinjuku-ku		electric range, refrigerator
	3-minute walk to Mejiro	Parking :	¥ 50,000 per car
	Station	Restrictions :	No pets
Floor space :	130 m², 5th floor		

How to Be a Happy Camper

Common renter blues

If you come to Japan, like where you stay, and like your neighbors, you'll like Japan. There are some problems that just can't be avoided when living in an apartment, but there are several things you can do to increase your chances of enjoying your stay.

Neighbors

Not many neighborhoods in Japan are used to foreigners, so depending on where you go, you might get curious looks when you move in. A good way to prevent problems is to visit your neighbors early on. A small gift like hand towels is appropriate. Here are some phrases for such occasions:

Watakushi wa John Davis *desu.*
⇨My name is John Davis.
London *kara kimashita.*
⇨I'm from London.
Tonari ni hikkoshite kimashita.
⇨I moved in next door.

Noise

If you're planning to have a let-your-hair-down evening, then it might be a good idea to give your neighbors fair warning. Be careful about rowdy parties as your Japanese neighbors tend to dislike noise at night.

Garbage

Non-Japanese in Japan have a reputation of not doing a good job of taking out the garbage. So doing it right can impress the neighbors. When, where and what kind of garbage on what days are all decided and vary by area — making it quite a science. Stick a memo on your refrigerator and live by it. (See p.28 Garbage Disposal)

Deposit

The deposit is always the No. 1 bone of contention between owners and foreign renters. Even with extreme care, wear and tear will happen, and when the real estate agent comes to do the final inspection, nothing will be overlooked. Consider yourself lucky if you get anything back.

Pets

If you found a pets-welcome apartment, regulations about pets are often in the contract. Obey the regulations to the letter, otherwise you will cause conflicts with neighbors. (See p.22 Pets)

Damage

Before signing the contract, look at the place to check for damage. If you find something, ask that it be repaired or at least documented. Inevitably, you'll notice something else after you move in, so let the agent know about it immediately so you don't have to pay to have it fixed.

When getting roommates

When you sign the apartment contract, you must include the names of everyone who will be living there. Before you let friends or relatives live with you, be sure to clear it with the real estate agent and owner.

Remodeling

Even something as simple as putting a nail in the wall can eat up your deposit. The return of your deposit is based on everything being the way it was when you got there, so think twice before doing anything. I once covered over a wall with nice paneling — I believed it was an improvement — but I had to pay for it when I moved out.

Size of the house

Everything about a Japanese apartment is probably smaller than what you're used to. This includes doorways — so think carefully before buying any big furniture. If you're tall, don't forget about the low doorframes.

Used furniture

Unless money is no issue or you're going to put down serious roots, buy used furniture. Most neighborhoods have shops where you can find used items like tables, sofas, and cabinets for far less than half of what you'd pay for new. I once bought a used cabinet with a very low 500-yen price tag, but to my untrained eyes it looked like an expensive antique. In Tokyo, the Salvation Army open bazaar on Saturday morning (03-3384-3769 Mon. to Fri.) offers used furniture as well as used clothes. Flea markets, classified ads in English newspapers and free papers, and the Internet are also great ways to find something to make your apartment more homey.

Pets

Keeping a pet in Japan

Japan can be a difficult place for people who like pets. Pets and pet supplies are expensive and most stores do not allow pets inside. If you do get a pet, one of your best sources of information will be your neighborhood veterinarian clinic. Here are some other things to think about.

Pets and landlords

First of all, make sure you get an apartment that allows pets — they're not easy to find. Fish, turtles, and maybe little birds are usually tolerated. But dogs and cats can cause enormous problems such as smells and noise. Even if pets are allowed, most apartment buildings will have a list of rules that you must obey.

Finding a pet in Japan

Having a pet in Japan is a luxury — you'll see why when you check the prices at pet stores. A little dachshund can easily cost more than 300,000 yen. Food and supplies also usually cost more than you are accustomed to. But if you can get away from the city centers and

shop at discount stores instead of specialized pet shops, prices become a little more reasonable.

A conscientious and inexpensive way to find a pet is to go to a shelter or a pet-rescue organization. The Internet offers many sites, some in English, where you can see photographs of pets in search of a home.

Legalities about dogs

When you get a dog from a pet shop or rescue center, you'll usually get information about registering your dog at the local government office. The fee is around 3,000 yen for tags and little stickers with the 犬 character to post at your doorway to warn visitors. Shots are required once a year. Your vet will have details.

You must file a notification with your local government office when your dog dies, or if there are changes in its registered information, like location or owner's name and address.

Out on the town

In the most urban areas, you must keep dogs under leash when you walk them. Dog dirt should be disposed of by the owner.

On trains and buses, policies differ by company, but usually pets must be kept in carriers, not leashed or in your lap. If you're very lucky, you'll find restaurants, coffee shops, and lodgings that welcome pets. Some coffee shops and restaurants even have special menus for well-behaved cats and dogs. Refer to the English Townpage (see p.40 SOS) for contact information. However, pets are generally not welcomed in places that sell food, so plan accordingly.

Taking vacations

Traveling with a pet can be stressful for all parties involved, especially cats and dogs. One option is to leave your pet at home and arrange to have someone come by, or maybe someone can take it home for a sleepover. Pet-sitter services are also available. You can also consider a pet hotel. Although rates vary, most offer excellent care. Your vet will have information.

Getting a pet in and out of Japan

Pets coming into Japan are quarantined for between 14 and 180 days to check for rabies and something called leptospirosis. The minimum time applies only when you have a proof-of-rabies vaccination and a health certificate.

When bringing a dog from an area of the world declared rabies free, the detention period can be as short as 12 hours. Make sure to get a health certificate from a government agency in your country. Quarantine stations are located at all the major airports and sea ports.

When you take a pet out of Japan, check with the Ministry of Agriculture, Forestry and Fisheries (http://www.animal-quarantine-service.go.jp/english/) or your vet. You'll need an inspection from your nearest Animal Quarantine Station for rabies and leptospirosis prior to departure, taking up to 12 hours of detention. You'll also want to find out all the requirements in the country you're going to.

Japanese-Style Houses

At home in Japan

The three major types of housing are individual houses, *manshons* (ferroconcrete or steel-framed apartment buildings; from the word mansion, but more like a condominium) and inexpensive apartments — some with no baths, but hopefully a public bath nearby. Most places will have both *washitsu*, Japanese-style rooms with *tatami* mats, and Western-style rooms with wood, tile, or carpeted flooring. In recent years, Japanese homes are becoming more and more Western, but overall, here is what you can expect.

Genkan (entrance)

Everyone knows shoes are not allowed in Japanese homes. When you enter, you'll find an area for removing shoes called the *genkan* before stepping up to the main level. In days past and still in the countryside, the woman of the house will greet visitors by kneeling on the elevated main floor and bowing to them. There will usually be slippers for guests to wear.

Bathrooms

Most homes now have Western-style toilets, but you'll still see a Japanese toilet now and then. It's basically porcelain trough. You use it by baring the appropriate parts of your body and squatting, facing the partial dome cover. In some of the older country homes, you may even have the choice experience of a no-flush toilet that is essentially a hole in the floor. Since you don't make contact, Japanese toilets are quite sanitary. Also note that the slippers in the bathroom are to be used nowhere else.

In most Japanese homes, the bathroom and toilet are separated. The bathrooms usually have showers next to or inside of the bathtub. The tubs aren't long enough to let you stretch out, but the neck-deep water certainly compensates. As others use the same hot water, wash off before you get in and don't get any soap inside the tub. Some homes use the same bath water for days.

Tatami mats

Made of straw around a center of foam mat or other material, making them about 5.5 cm thick. A lot of straw was used in times past, but more chemical materials are used nowadays. Each *tatami*, which is about 180 by 90 centimeters or a little smaller, is also how the size of rooms are commonly measured. So a room that is 6 *tatami* is 9.72 square meters. New t*atami* are light green and give off a pleasant smell. They should be changed every few years or whenever someone moves. A *tatami* room really makes you feel like you're in Japan. Slippers are left outside *tatami* rooms.

Shōji and fusuma

These are the sliding doors between rooms. A *shōji* is made of latticed wooden frames covered on one side with *shōji* paper. *Fusuma* is a thicker door with paper on both sides. These doors can often be removed to open up two rooms and make them appear as one. You can usually replace the *shōji* paper by yourself, but it takes a specialist to redo *fusuma*.

Tokonoma

This is a small, slightly elevated space usually in the corner of *tatami* rooms. It's where Japanese would perhaps display a *kakejiku* scroll painting or flower arrangement. At present, *tokonoma* have disappeared from most of modern houses and apartments.

Oshiire

You know that the Japanese bed is a *futon* (mattress and comforter in a pair), and so instead of making their beds, Japanese put away their *futon* in a closet with sliding doors called *oshiire* — an essential part of every *tatami*-covered room.

Jō and *tsubo*

House floor area is frequently shown in three ways, square meters, *jō* and *tsubo*. One *jō* is a *tatami* mat, about 180 cm x 90 cm. One *tsubo* is 182 cm x 182 cm or about 3.3 m² and equals approximately two *jō*. Beware that listed areas include the bathroom, kitchen and closets.

Earthquake Readiness

Not if but when

Earthquakes in Japan are a daily occurrence, but most are nothing to panic about. The government has taken various measures to reduce the effect of earthquakes, but you also need to collect the basic information and get personally prepared.

Before an earthquake

Many local governments will have English information about disaster preparation. If you are a member of the Chamber of Commerce of your country, you can also get information from its homepage. Such information will give you a wide range of suggestions, but everyone needs to have an earthquake survival kit that includes; drinking water and emergency food for two or three days, first-aid supplies, flashlights and a portable radio with extra batteries.

There's nothing you can do about the severity of an earthquake, but you can help limit the damage.

— Do not place heavy objects in high places were they might fall.

— Purchase and install devices such as expandable steel poles that go between large furniture and the ceiling, wedges to lean furniture against the wall, and stoppers to keep cupboards from opening.

— Do not place any objects where they can fall and block hallways or exits.

— Disaster Prevention Day on September 1 is the time for neighborhood disaster drills. If you participate, you'll get an idea of what you should do.

— Have a fire extinguisher, know where it is, and know how to use it. Many neighborhoods have public extinguishers, too.

— Know where the evacuation area is for your neighborhood.

— If you live on the second floor or higher,

make sure you have an emergency escape ladder or other means of getting out of the building when the normal methods are blocked.

During an earthquake

When a big earthquake hits, don't panic! Stay calm and think carefully about what has to be done first. What you do will depend on the situation, but here are a few guidelines:

— Turn off all gas valves. Douse any flames and do not light matches or lighters. Fires after an earthquake can be much more dangerous than the actual temblor.

— Don't run outside. It is generally best to stay inside and take cover in a doorway or under a table.

— Move away from windows, mirrors and other glass. Try to get away from chest-of-drawers, TVs, and other heavy furniture that might topple over on you.

— If you're in a car, stop at the side of the road where you won't block emergency vehicles.

After an earthquake

When the shaking stops, evaluate your situation and choose a course of action. Here are some possibilities.

— Never be influenced by rumors. If you live in Tokyo, Kanagawa, Chiba, Saitama area, tune the radio to InterFM in Tokyo for information. In the Osaka area, FM-YY provides multi-language broadcasting. If you have an i-mode mobile telephone, you'll be able to get the latest bulletins in English from news services such as CNN, Nikkei News and Asahi Shimbun. For details visit: http://www.nttdocomo.com/

— Turn off electricity, main gas and water valves when possible, and leave the building if you smell anything or suspect further damage from aftershocks.

— Avoid using cars so the roads can stay open to emergency vehicles.

— Along the coast, get to high ground to save yourself from tidal waves.

G o o d *to* **k n o w** ··

- ●じしん [*jishin*] ▷ earthquake
- ●しんど [*shindo*] ▷ magnitude
- ●だいじしん [*dai-jishin*] ▷ large earthquake
- ●よしん [*yoshin*] ▷ aftershock
- ●つなみ [*tsunami*] ▷ tidal wave
- ●かじ [*kaji*] ▷ fire
- ●たすけて！ [*Tasukete!*] ▷ Help!
- ●だいじょうぶ。 [*Daijōbu.*] ▷ I'm okay.
- ●だいじょうぶですか？ [*Daijōbu desu ka?*] ▷ Are you okay?

Garbage Disposal

The fine art of taking out the garbage

Taking care of the garbage may be the least of your worries, but to your Japanese neighbors, it's a high priority. In fact, improper garbage disposal ranks high on the list of gripes Japanese have about their non-Japanese neighbors. So if you want to develop friendly relations with your neighbors, find out the local requisites for garbage disposal. Then do it right.

Learn the garbage facts

When you go to register at the city or ward office, it's a good idea to ask for information about how to take out the garbage. Usually, they can explain the details or give a list to you. There are signs at the garbage collection sites that give the details about what garbage is collected on which days, but seldom in English. When you move into a new place, get the landlord or a helpful neighbor to give you the rundown.

Each neighborhood and each city in Japan has different rules, but here is some of what you'll need to know in Tokyo, which has some of the stricter rules around.

How?

Use translucent plastic bags for everything except recyclable garbage. You can get ten for around 100 yen at any convenience store.

When?

There is one recyclable waste day (*shi-gen-gomi no hi*), one incombustible waste day (*moenai gomi no hi*), and two combustible waste days (*moeru gomi no hi*) in a week. Garbage is collected in the morning and should be put out by around 8:00, but avoid putting it out the night before. Otherwise you may wake up to see your personal life spread across the neighborhood by the crows. Be careful, there may be no garbage pick-up on holidays.

Where?

Put your garbage only in designated locations. They're usually marked with a sign, but not much more. Condominiums may have their own garbage collection areas.

What's recyclable?

Old newspapers, magazines, and cardboard — tie them up in stacks with string. Aluminum cans and bottles — rinse them out with water before placing them in the separate containers at the collection area on recycle days.

PET bottles should probably be carried to your local convenience stores where there're containers for them. That way, they're sure to get recycled instead of put in a landfill. Many supermarkets also have collection boxes for PET bottles and Styrofoom trays to be recycled. You'll need to take off the lid (incombustible) and smash the bottle flat with your foot.

Electric appliances such as washing machine, refrigerator, air-conditioner and TV (only cathode-ray tube type) must be recyclable. The shop where you bought them or your local office will have information.

What about the stuff that burns?

In Tokyo, this includes kitchen garbage, wastepaper, wood, clothes and disposable diapers.

And the stuff that doesn't burn?

This includes metal, glass, ceramics, plastic, rubber and leather. Don't put spray cans in the incombustibles bag. Carry them out and put them on the ground by themselves so the garbage collectors can handled properly.

How about the really big stuff?

Don't put your old furniture or appliances out on the street. For that and anything else too big to fit in a garbage bag, you'll need to call the sanitation department to have a special truck sent around. Ask a Japanese-speaking friend to tell them what it is and the size, and they'll tell you how much it's going to cost. They'll either bill you for it or you can buy fee stickers at convenience stores.

And garbage from business activities?

In Tokyo and other cities, both companies and individuals pay to have their garbage hauled away. Stickers are purchased at convenience stores and placed on the translucent garbage bags with the name of the company.

G o o d to k n o w ....

- ●ごみしゅうしゅう [gomi shūshū]   ▷ garbage collection
- ●もえるごみ [moeru gomi]   ▷ combustible garbage
- ●もえないごみ [moenai gomi]   ▷ incombustible waste
- ●リサイクル [risaikuru]   ▷ recycle
- ●ごみしゅうせきじょ [gomi-shūsekijo]   ▷ garbage collection location
- ●そだいごみ [sodai-gomi]   ▷ large garbage

Public Services

Getting your tax's worth

One of the easiest and least-expensive ways to enjoy your time in Japan is to use public services. You'll find a variety of services in your neighborhood, either free or very inexpensive. Your local city office will have all the details for your neighborhood, but here are some of the things to look for.

Consultation services

Many local government offices offer free consultation in English and other languages that can help you with a surprising range of problems, either by phone or face-to-face. Check the number of the consultation service of your local office from English Townpage. (See p.40 SOS) Typical issues dealt with are problems with neighbors, unpaid wages, and medical care. They can also inform you about government subsidies, international exchange opportunities, and cultural classes, just to name a few. If they don't have the answer to your question, they can usually tell you where to go.

Disaster preparedness

Local governments are charged with assisting after disasters — earthquake, torrential rains, and typhoons. They have a great deal of the information for you, including official evacuation site locations, first aid, medical supplies, telecommunication devices, radio systems, electric generators, water, and food. Another thing: besides responding to fires and accidents, fire departments operate the ambulance service.

Public sports centers

Most major cities have nice sports clubs, but public swimming pools and gyms are an economical option. Public sports centers also offer a variety of sports classes ranging from aerobics to archery and judo to free climbing. There may be more than one sports center operated by local governments nearby, so with a little investigation you should be able to find something. And you'll pay much less to do what you want to do than by purchasing a membership at a sports club. You can get information on sports centers from your local city office.

Recycle centers

Some local governments operate recycle centers that have nice recycled furniture and other items at very reasonable prices. Some have bidding systems, others sell things off the shelf.

Community Centers

Many local governments run neighborhood cultural facilities, *shimin bunka kaikan, kumin sentā,* and *kōminkan* being the more common types. Most will offer classes such as Japanese painting, karate, flower arranging and calligraphy for free or for the cost of materials. A friend of mine improved her spoken Japanese considerably by taking free lessons in Japanese sign language. Lessons at cultural centers are a great way to make friends, too. Most cities also operate museums and concert halls.

Libraries

Finding a library in Japan isn't difficult; finding one with a large collection of English material is a challenge. You can register at any public library (not just the one where you live or work) and most will have some English newspapers and magazines. Some lend out music CDs, tapes, and even computer software.

Libraries, English-speakers will want to know about are the American Center Reference Service (03-3436-0901), the British Council Library (03-3235-8031), the Japan Foundation Library (03-5562-3527), and the Tokyo Central Metropolitan Library (03-3442-8451).

Useful telephone numbers

●Consultation Services
[Tokyo]
Tokyo Metropolitan Government Foreign Residents' Advisory Center
        03-5320-7744
(9:30-12:00 a.m. and 1:00-4:00 p.m., weekdays)
[Osaka]
Osaka Information Service for Foreign Residents   06-6941-2297
(9:00 a.m.-5:30 p.m., weekdays)

●Embassies
Australian Embassy	03-5232-4111
Embassy of Canada	03-5412-6200
Embassy of India	03-3262-2391
British Embassy	03-5211-1100
Embassy of the United States of America	03-3224-5000

The Post Office

How to send your very best

E-mail has not completely replaced snail-mail and so you'll want to know the basics. The first thing is to find a post office — just look for a building with the 〒 symbol. They are open from 9:00 a.m. to 5:00 p.m. on Monday to Friday. But larger post offices keep longer hours, and some are open mornings of Saturday and Sunday.

Domestic mail

Postage fees: 50 yen for postcards and 80 yen for normal envelopes.

Express Delivery: If you're in a hurry, *sokutatsu* (速達 express delivery) is available at your local post office. If you put on the correct postage and put a red mark across one end of the envelope, you don't even have to go to the post office.

Registered mail: For those really important documents, ask for *kakitome* (書留 registered mail) at the post office. Lost registered mail is compensated. Use *genkin kakitome* (現金書留) for sending cash. It's a convenient registered mail service for sending money, as checks are uncommon in Japan.

International mail

Aerograms: 90 yen at any post office.

Small parcels: Packages under 2kg are handled as small parcels. Special custom's declaration seal must be filled out and attached at the post office.

Other services

Moving notification: Fill out an *iten-todoke* (moving notification) postcard at the post office so your mail can be sent to your new address for one year. By that time you should have notified everyone of your new address.

Special delivery notification: If you're not at home when a package or other special delivery mail arrives, the carrier will leave a notification postcard called *fuzai tsūchi*. Either call for redelivery or fill in a date when you'll be home and send in the postcard. You can also take the card and your ID to the post office to get the item.

Long absences: Notify the post office and they'll hold your mail for 30 days.

More detailed information is available at the Post Office Home Page. (http://www.post.yusei.go.jp/new-eng/index.htm)
Postal Services Information in English (Monday - Friday, 9:30 a.m.-4:30 p.m.)
Tokyo: 03-5472-5851～2
Osaka: 06-6944-6245

ぎんこう

The Bank

Money smart

In Japan, cash does most of the talking. Credit cards are making headway, and you'll have few problems finding places to use them. But cash is still king. So it's a good thing that there's either a bank or an ATM machine on nearly every street corner.

Take a number and wait. It's the first thing you'll need to do when you enter a bank. You'll wait for a long time especially on payday. Teller windows are open from 9:00 a.m. to 3:00 p.m.

Savings accounts require your foreign registration card to open. Most Japanese use a personal stamp called a *hanko*, but you can also use your signature. One thousand yen is enough to open an account.

Automatic teller machines are available almost everywhere. Their hours are usually 8:45 a.m. to 7:00 p.m. There are no 24-hour ATMs at Japanese banks. But some are open on Saturday mornings. Money can be withdrawn from any ATM, but a small fee is charged when you use the ATM of a bank where you don't have an account. ATMs at major banks have instructions in English.

You can also withdraw money at the ATMs of convenience stores.

Automatic payment is possible for taxes, insurance fees, NHK television fees, telephone fees, rent, and so on. Most companies will also deposit your salary into your account, although cash is still common among smaller companies.

G o o d *to* k n o w ....

- ●よきん [*yokin*]　▷ deposit
- ●よきんこうざ [*yokin kōza*]　▷ bank account
- ●キャッシュカード [*kyasshu kādo*]　▷ cash card
- ●クレジットカード [*kurejitto kādo*]　▷ credit card
- ●きんり [*kinri*]　▷ interest

[税金] *zeikin*

Taxes

Tax facts

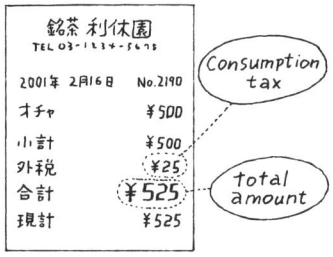

The tax system in Japan is complicated. But if you work for a company, you don't have to worry about filing taxes because the accounting department does the messy paperwork. If you have to file your tax by yourself, the local government and National Tax Agency are always there to help. Foreign businesspeople in Japan need to be concerned mainly about three types of taxes.

Consumption tax *(shōhi-zei)*

The consumption tax on most purchases is five percent. Some items like stamps, prepaid cards and resident's card fees are tax-free.

Income tax *(shotoku-zei)*

Income taxes are deducted from your salary. They are also called withholding tax *(gensen-chōshū)*. When offered a job, make sure you know if the salary is before or after taxes. At the end of the year, if you submit such documents as insurance certificates, number of dependents, to the general affairs department of your company, an adjustment will be made and the extra returned. The self-employed must file their own tax returns.

Resident's tax *(jūmin-zei)*

Resident's taxes are based on your national tax returns for the previous year, and so can't be assessed until after

you've filed one. When you return to your native country, you may find you owe taxes for the current year.

By when

If you are self-employed, have an income over a certain level, or make money in addition to your normal salary, file between February 16 and March 15 and pay if necessary by March 15. If you're headed home, pay before getting on the plane.

Where to go for help

Tokyo Regional Taxation Bureau
03-3821-9070
Nagoya Regional Taxation Bureau
052-971-2059

G o o d *to* k n o w ···

- ●ぜいむしょ [*zeimusho*]   ▷ tax office
- ●ねんまつちょうせい [*nemmatsu chōsei*]   ▷ year-end adjustment
- ●てどりしゅうにゅう [*tedori shūnyū*]   ▷ after-tax income
- ●かくていしんこく [*kakutei shinkoku*]   ▷ final tax returns

Health Insurance

Don't be caught without it

There are two types of public health insurance in Japan; employee's health insurance schemes and the national health insurance scheme. Persons who live in Japan for over one year are required to enroll in one type or the other. Foreign medical insurance policies are not valid in Japan.

Company employees will be enrolled an employee's health insurance scheme (*shakai hoken*). Usually the personnel department handles the paper work.

National health insurance (*kokumin kenkō hoken*) is for the self-employed and others who are not covered by an employee's health insurance scheme. Enroll at the National Health Insurance section of your local city office. You'll need to bring your foreign registration card with you. You'll receive an insurance card called *hokenshō* to show you are insured.

The insurance premium is calculated on a per-year basis. The year runs from April through March and is based on your income in Japan for the previous year and on the number of family members. The premium and the ways to calculate it vary with each local government. Ask the National Health Insurance section at your local city government office for more details.

At the clinic or hospital, you will need to **pay before leaving**, so make sure you have your insurance card and be prepared to pay the **co-payment**, 20-30 percent of the bill.

Any type of elective surgery or procedure like medical checkups, immunizations, cosmetic surgery, and normal birth will not be covered. So try to be as informed as possible and ask lots of questions about what procedures are to be performed.

G o o d *to* k n o w ....

- ●けんこうほうけんせいど [*kenkō hoken seido*] ▷ health insurance system
- ●ほけんりょう [*hokenryō*] ▷ insurance premium
- ●じこふたん [*jiko futan*] ▷ co-payment
- ●いりょうひ [*iryōhi*] ▷ fee for medical treatment
- ●しゃかいほけん [*shakai hoken*] ▷ social insurance

Health Care

Taking care of yourself

Whenever going to the hospital or a clinic for the first time, make sure you take your insurance card (*hokenshō*), some form of identification, and some cash — no credit cards. If you're going back, you'll also need an examination card (*shinsatsuken*), which may have the time and date of your next appointment, and more cash.

Get in line

Doctor appointments are generally non-existent in Japan and walk-ins are usually accepted only in the morning, especially in the general hospitals. When you arrive at the hospital or clinic, first visit the reception desk. They'll ask you to fill out forms. From there you might be sent to a smaller waiting room to wait before the doctor calls you into the examination room. When your examination is done, you'll be handed some papers that you'll need to return to the reception desk. After waiting some more, they'll call you to the counter where you can make your payment.

Take your medicine

Insurance covers most prescription drug costs. Your out-of-pocket payment is generally between 100 and 200 yen for each prescription. Prescriptions are usually filled by a pharmacy. Some doctors tend to prescribe several medicines for the smallest of problems.

Japanese medicine will not have instructions in English, so ask lots of questions. About half of the medicine comes in powder instead of pill form, so make sure you have lots of water on hand.

So where's the drugstore?

There are two types of drugstores — those that fill prescriptions and those that sell non-prescription medicine. You won't have any trouble finding a non-prescription drugstore except late at night. Almost none are open 24 hours, some convenience stores do sell a few simple remedies like aspirin. It's always a good idea to have common drugs and medical supplies on hand.

Does anyone speak English?

Finding a doctor or specialist who speaks English is no easy task. The English pages of Internet sites for most major cities will list English-speaking medical resources. For both routine and emergency care, you can probably find someone who speaks your language at a public hospital or a large private hospital.

Private hospitals

Tokyo has four large private hospitals that have English speaking staff: Japanese Red Cross Medical Center (03-3400-1311), Tokyo Medical and Surgical Clinic (03-3436-3028), St. Luke's International Hospital (03-3541-5151),

and International Catholic Hospital (03-3951-1111). In other cities, you might want to talk with your consulate.

At the dentists

Dental procedures covered by insurance are limited and those not covered are expensive. Ask around and you should be able to find a competent Western-trained dentist without too much difficulty. You can find information on English-speaking dentists in English newspapers, free papers, and the English Townpage. (See p.40 SOS)

Be sure to have the dentist explain thoroughly what needs to be done and make your own decision as to what you will have done and what you choose to let go. Dentists are paid by the health insurance system for every visit you make, so expect several visits to complete even simple procedures. On the positive side, most dentists let you make appointments.

G o o d *to* k n o w ······················

- ●ねつがある。[Netsu ga aru.]
- ●おなかがいたい。[Onaka ga itai.]
- ●きもちがわるい。[Kimochi ga warui.]
- ●あたまがいたい。[Atama ga itai.]
- ●のどがいたい。[Nodo ga itai.]
- ●せきがとまらない。[Seki ga tomaranai.]
- ●めまいがする。[Memai ga suru.]
- ●けがをしました。[Kega o shimashita.]
- ●ちがとまらない。[Chi ga tomaranai.]

- ▷ I have a fever.
- ▷ My stomach hurts.
- ▷ I feel bad.
- ▷ I have a headache.
- ▷ I have a sore throat.
- ▷ I can't stop coughing.
- ▷ I feel dizzy.
- ▷ I've been injured.
- ▷ The bleeding won't stop.

Telecommunications

Call someone who cares

In crowded commuter trains, you might be surprised to see many people leaning their heads forward, moving their thumbs rapidly while gazing at their cellular phones. Cell phones evolve on a daily basis, getting more compact and gaining multiple functions such as information services and e-mail capabilities. Price schemes vary among cell phones and telephones, so be properly informed and you can pay less.

Cellular phones

There are now more people in Japan with cellular phones (*keitai denwa*) than regular telephone lines. With some form of ID and a bank account, you can be talking away within a few hours. The two types are the regular cellular phone and the less-expensive PHS phone, each with various options — some allowing for international calls. The PHS works great in the cities, but not so well elsewhere. Some new-generation cellular phones have functions like those of a computer.

A phone of your own

To get a telephone line, take your passport or foreign registration card to an NTT office. A simple telephone connection will usually be around 70,000 yen depending on what options you get. You can buy a used line from someone leaving the country for much less. For the short term, you may consider renting a line, but it might not let you make international calls. Once you get your line, you must get a telephone at an electronics store. Call charges vary with the time of day, so ask the telephone companies for details — they're all very foreigner-friendly. And rates are going down.

Public telephones

You'll find public phones (*kōshū denwa*) almost anywhere you go. Most will take 10-yen coins, 100-yen coins, and telephone cards which are sold at convenience stores and other places in units of 500 and 1,000 yen. Just stick whatever you have in the slot and dial. Local calls cost 10 yen for one minute. For long distance, you'll want telephone cards. Otherwise you'll have to bring a bucketful of 10-yen coins or a handful of 100-yen coins — no change. The newer gray telephones have ISDN modular jacks where you can hook up your portable computer and do e-mail. Most of the newer public phones have instructions in English.

International calls

International calls (*kokusai denwa*) can be made through private telephones or pay phones with an international mark. For international pay-phone calls, use telephone cards or 100-yen coins (some phones also take credit cards). The KDD Super World Card, available in 1,000, 3,000 and 5,000 yen units, can be purchased at most convenience stores. There are several international telephone companies with varying prices, so it's worth some investigation.

Most hotel rooms are equipped with analogue telephone lines. Direct international telephone calls are usually possible. Internet access is possible from many hotel rooms.

Call-back systems

One way to get around the high prices of an international phone call in Japan is to register for a call-back system. With most systems, you dial a number, enter a long list of numbers, and then you get a call back that connects you. This allows you to cut your telephone bill by as much as two-thirds. Most of the English newspapers will have advertisements. Internet phones are another alternative.

G o o d *to* **k n o w** ·

- ●るすばんでんわ [*rusuban denwa*]　▷ answering machine
- ●かいぎでんわ [*kaigi denwa*]　▷ conference call
- ●ないせん [*naisen*]　▷ extension
- ●しがいきょくばん [*shigai kyokuban*]　▷ long-distance number
- ●でんわきょく [*denwa-kyoku*]　▷ telephone company
- ●でんわちょう [*denwa-chō*]　▷ telephone directory
- ●でんわばんごう [*denwa bangō*]　▷ telephone number

SOS

Where to go for help

If you get in serious trouble in Japan, get help. Even if you're the self-sufficient type, there are professionals to help with almost any problem you face. Having someone to help you overcome the language barrier will greatly increase your options. The contact information here is mainly for the Tokyo area, but most of these numbers will be able to provide you information about where you can get help locally.

Emergency calls

Nationwide, call 110 to report a crime; to report a traffic accident or fire, call 119. Operators are on duty, around the clock. First let the operator know — Japanese or slow and calm English — if you're reporting a traffic accident (*kotsū jiko*) or fire (*kaji*), or need an ambulance (*kyūkyūsha*), and then give the address and details of the situation.

While at home waiting for the ambulance, try to find a Japanese speaking person to accompany non-Japanese speaking patients and also prepare the patient's passport, foreign registration card, cash, and insurance cards. When the ambulance arrives, send someone outside to meet it.

Emergency numbers can be called from most public phones at no charge by pushing an emergency call button or by dialing 110 or 119. From cellular or PHS phones, call 110 or 119 without an area code.

You may be called back for details about the emergency, so leave your number and try to remain available for at least 10 minutes.

If you're involved in a traffic accident, be sure to get information such as name, address, and occupation of the other party. Get the vehicle registration number and insurance company names. To get the Traffic Accident Certificate that your insurance company requires, you'll need to fill out a police report.

Lost & found

There's an excellent chance that you'll get your lost wallet or purse back. It's a widely accepted practice to take found items to the police station as soon as possible. I once got a postcard from the police telling me that the wallet I'd lost three months earlier had been found — everything intact. If you leave something in the trains or at the station, ask someone at the station to help you that same day.

Counseling services

Many city offices also offer free and confidential counseling services in English and other languages. It's a good idea to keep their telephone number and that of other sources of help with you when going out.

Call Tokyo English Life Line (03-3968-4099) for free and confidential counseling 9:00 a.m. to 4:00 p.m. and 7:00 to 11:00 p.m. Their website is at <http://www.tell.gol.com>.

Townpage

One of the most valuable publications is the English Townpage — Japan's version of Yellow Pages. For a copy, drop by any NTT office, check out their Internet site (http://english.townpage.isp.ntt.co.jp/) or call 0120-460815. An East Japan Edition and a West Japan Edition are available. In the Townpage, you'll find a variety of English-speaking health care services that include acupuncture, psychotherapy, dieting, cosmetic surgery and dermatology, holistic counseling, family counseling, and eye surgery.

Good to know

- かじです。 [Kaji desu.] ▷ There's a fire.
- きゅうびょうです。 [Kyūbyō desu.] ▷ There's been a sudden illness.
- けがです。 [Kega desu.] ▷ I'm injured.
- こうつうじこです。 [Kōtsū jiko desu.] ▷ There's a traffic accident.
- ごうとうです。 [Gōtō desu.] ▷ There's been a robbery.
- わたしのなまえは…。 [Watashi no namae wa ...] ▷ My name is ...
- わたしのじゅうしょは…。 [Watashi no jūsho wa ...] ▷ My address is ...
- わたしのでんわばんごうは…。 [Watashi no denwa bangō wa ...] ▷ My telephone number is ...
- にほんごができません。 [Nihongo ga dekimasen.] ▷ I can't speak Japanese.
- こうばんはどこですか？ [Kōban wa doko desu ka?] ▷ Where is the police box?
- さいふをなくしました。 [Saifu o nakushimashita.] ▷ I lost my wallet.

[何を食べますか] なに た *nani o tabemasu ka*

Feeling Hungry?

Finding something to eat

How much you like the food in Japan will be an accurate barometer of how you like your stay. Based on an informal survey of foreigners living in Japan, here is a list of foods you'll want to try and maybe some that you'll want to avoid.

Five best-liked foods

1. *Rāmen*: If you're used to instant *rāmen* noodles sold around the world, then you should try real *rāmen*. The Japanese have perfected delicious *rāmen* for almost every taste.

2. Curry: You'll find all kinds of curry and rice with a variety of ingredients. The Japanese version of this Indian dish is quick, tasty and inexpensive, making it a favorite for Japanese and non-Japanese at home and on the go.

3. *Tempura*: *Tempura* is something like deep-fried onion rings. Instead of catsup, you dip the *tempura* in a shoyu (soy sauce)-based sauce or salt. *Tempura*

ingredients by the way, include shrimp, squid, fish and all kinds of vegetables.

4. *Shabu-shabu*: This is basically thin slices of meat, tofu, mushrooms and vegetables in a light soup. The boiling soup pot is placed in the middle of the table and everyone cooks their own slices of meat at their own pace by dangling each one in the soup for just long enough for it to change color. The cooked meat is then dipped in a soy or sesame seed based sauce and eaten.

5. *Gyōza*: The usual translation is dumpling, but they are basically minced pork and vegetables wrapped in a thin dough, and either fried or boiled. Fried *gyōza* are peculiar in Japan and they taste crispy outside, and juicy on the inside! It's pretty hard not to like them.

Five least-liked foods

Here are the foods that non-Japanese least want to take home in their suitcases, but don't let this stop you from trying something new and different.

1. *Nattō*: It's basically fermented beans that look and smell like something left in the back of the refrigerator for much too long. But don't take my word for it — some foreigners actually do like it. Packed full of calcium and other nutrients, *nattō* is also one of the healthiest things you can eat.

2. *Umeboshi*: *Umeboshi* is pickled plum, but that doesn't quite explain it. They are usually dyed red with perilla leaves, and so salty and sour they make your mouth pucker. Japanese will often eat one *umeboshi* with one bowl of rice. Since it contains citric acid, it is good for sterilization of other food and for recovering from fatigue.

3. *Kaiseki-ryōri*: This is the kind of food served at tea ceremonies to get the participants to the next meal, so it consists of all sorts of little dishes with even smaller portions of vegetarian food, like three little beans on a leaf. Take your camera, but have something to eat first. Each of the dishes are really good but probably not enough to fill your stomach.

4. Japanese pickles: Japanese pickles (*tsukemono*) are made from just about any kind of vegetable — some are rather tasty. The one that attracts the most negative attention by foreigners is called *takuan*, a white radish dyed bright yellow and served with many Japanese meals.

5. *Anko*: Usually translated as "sweet bean paste," *anko* is a main ingredient in many Japanese desserts. If you're used to eating salty beans like those in Mexican chili, then you're in for a shock. In fact, sweet is the main way to eat beans in Japan.

As you can see, the food in the second list is healthier and lower in fat. Take your pick.

- ● おはし [*ohashi*] ▷ chopsticks
- ● ちゃわん [*chawan*] ▷ rice bowl
- ● ごはん [*gohan*] ▷ rice (also refers to meals)
- ● あさごはん [*asa gohan*] ▷ breakfast
- ● ひるごはん [*hiru gohan*] ▷ lunch
- ● ばんごはん [*ban gohan*] ▷ dinner
- ● レストラン [*resutoran*] ▷ restaurant
- ● みそしる [*misoshiru*] ▷ soybean paste soup
- ● しょうゆ [*shōyu*] ▷ soy sauce

Out to Lunch

Simple and delicious

Lunchtime in Japan is usually noon to 1:00 p.m.—an hour. Businesspeople rush to the restaurants and some get as crowded as rush-hour trains. There are so many restaurants and food outlets near most business centers that you can find exactly the right place to fit your mood, budget, taste or timetable. Here's a rundown of some choices.

Teishoku at *Izakaya*

A *teishoku* is a combination meal that usually comes with a main dish, rice, soup, pickles, and maybe something to drink. A lot of *izakaya* will serve only several kinds of *teishoku,* including *higawari teishoku* (daily meal), during the lunch hour. Prices are generally around 1,000 yen. And at most places you pay as you leave.

Specialized restaurants — Japanese, non-Japanese

Included in this category is a wide variety of low-priced sushi shops, curry (not technically Japanese), and noodle shops. Noodle shops are about the most common type of eatery in Japan. In addi-

tion to *rāmen,* you'll also find buckwheat *soba* noodles and *udon,* the thicker noodles made from white flour. Both *soba* and *udon* come either hot or cold with a soup that you dip the noodles in just before you eat them. You can usually get a decent meal for 1,000 yen or less.

Japan also has a variety of Italian, French, Chinese, Asian and American-style restaurants. While prices vary, for less than 2,000 yen you can usually find something that tastes great. Some non-Japanese food even tastes better in Japan than in its home country.

Tachigui

This is the mother of cheap food in Japan. For 500 yen or less you can get a bowl of noodles, curry and rice, or a beef bowl — and fast. But there are no chairs to sit on, just a counter to stand at. Most require that you buy a ticket from a machine at the entrance or pay when your food is served. It might be better to go with a Japanese friend the first time.

Family restaurants

The term "family restaurant" refers to Western-looking restaurants that serve both Western and Japanese foods. There are several chains such as Skylark, Denny's and Jonathan's. You'll probably pay a little over 1,000 yen to get filled up, but most family restaurants are clean and the service is good. Many places will have a daily special (*higawari* lunch) that may include all-you-can-drink coffee and tea. Some are open 24 hours.

Western fast food shops

McDonald's, KFC, Wendy's, Shakey's ... Hamburgers, pizza, and fried chicken, you'll find just about anything that you'll find at a shopping mall back

home, although prices may be a little higher than what you're used to.

Bentō (box lunch)

One of the most common forms of lunch is the *bentō*, an all-in-one meal, usually in a box. Around lunchtime in the office districts, you'll usually see long lines form in front of the *bentō* stands located seemingly on most every corner. Prices generally run from 300 to 1,000 yen. And you can buy them at convenience stores, too. Or you can bring one from home if you have someone to make it for you.

Demae (delivery services)

Most small restaurants in Japan offer delivery services that are quick and usually the same price as for eat-in. *Rāmen*, *soba* and sushi restaurants, as well as pizza, deliver hot food at your request. You shouldn't have any problem finding take-out menus that you can keep handy so you can call when you feel like staying in.

When you want to eat a lot

Many restaurants — some higher class and in hotels — offer all-you-can-eat buffets ranging from about 800 to 3,000 yen, drinks and desserts included. The term in Japanese is "*tabehōdai*" or "Viking." It's a great way to get a good look at the food before you put it on your plate.

Another fad is large-portion challenges for those who can never seem to get enough. Eat three jumbo *rāmen*, five bowls of curry and rice, or 60 *gyōza* within in the time limit and you can get your meal for free — fail and you pay the full price. Those who participate in this type of self-torture on a regular basis are called "food fighters."

Kaiten-zushi

Sushi on the run

Restaurants featuring sushi on a conveyor belt that moves in front of you have appeared across Europe and the United States. If you've tried *kaiten-zushi* outside of Japan, you may find that it's quite a bit different when you try one here. There are at least one or two *kaiten-zushi* shops near most train stations — especially handy when you want to catch a bite before catching a train.

The system

Customers sit along a circulating conveyor belt lined with small plates of sushi and simply pick up whatever they want. In the center stand the sushi cooks putting various kinds of toppings on little bite-sized rice with *wasabi* or Japanese horseradish — more on this later. At some places, the price is the same for all dishes, while at others, a different color or shape of plate means a different price. The lowest prices are generally around 130 yen, while more expensive plates may be around 400 yen.

Some of the sushi, usually two pieces to a plate, may look familiar, like tuna fish sandwich filling on rice, while others look more like fish eggs — red caviar if

you may. With around 40 different types — three-quarters are uncooked fish — you're bound to find something you really like.

If you want to order something that's not on the conveyor belt, just say like, "*Maguro, kudasai* (Tuna, please)."

After you've had your fill, simply stand up and someone will come around to count the number of plates you've emptied.

On the safe side

Sushi dining is considered safe even if the fish is not cooked. And there are two things you can do for extra safety — both greens. First, don't scrape off the *wasabi* even though you may first react to it like you would to a hot pepper — you may even learn to like it. And drink the green tea. Take a cup, usually kept above the conveyor belt, toss in a tea bag, maybe two, and then get hot water from the tap in front of you. The taste of sushi can be quite subtle, so Japanese sip the tea between bites so they can better enjoy the flavors, but the tea also kills germs. The thin pink slices of pickled ginger called *gari* are another means of clearing your mouth.

Another precaution is to choose shops that are crowded so that you don't get something that's already gone around the conveyor belt several times. Some people watch the sushi cooks and then pick up only the plates that they actually see being placed on the conveyor belt.

Sushi etiquette

The proper way to eat sushi is with your hands. Hold the sides between your thumb and middle finger and put your index finger over the top like you're pushing a button. Then turn it over and dip the morsel on the top in soy sauce. But proper isn't always what you like. To get more soy sauce on your sushi, just hold it with chopsticks and dip it in, rice first. It usually holds together long enough to get it in your mouth.

G o o d *to* k n o w ······················

There are three ways to write sushi in Japanese; 「すし」「寿司」「鮨」.

<Raw fish>
- ●まぐろ [*maguro*] ▷ tuna (fatty flesh of tuna is called *toro* とろ)
- ●かつお [*katsuo*] ▷ bonito
- ●いか [*ika*] ▷ squid, cuttlefish
- ●えび [*ebi*] ▷ shrimp
- ●いくら [*ikura*] ▷ salmon roe
- ●ほたて [*hotate*] ▷ scallop

<For those who don't go for raw>
- ●あなご [*anago*] ▷ conger eel
- ●たまご [*tamago*] ▷ sweet egg custard
- ●かっぱまき [*kappa-maki*] ▷ cucumber roll

<Other sushi terms>
- ●がり [*gari*] ▷ vinegared ginger
- ●しょうゆ [*shōyu*] ▷ soy sauce
- ●わさび [*wasabi*] ▷ Japanese horseradish
- ●あがり [*agari*] ▷ The green tea provided when you're finished eating.

Grocery Shopping

Finding good to eat

Shopping for food in Japan is a cultural experience in itself. Some stores specialize in imported foods, but they may charge you double what you'd pay at home. You could also try some of the Japanese foods at your local supermarket; they cost less. In the suburbs, shopping malls are the most convenient, but neighborhoods in residential areas still have shopping streets where you can go from one store to another to do your shopping.

Rice (*kome*)

Rice is the staple food in Japan, though it's not as cheap as you might expect. Anyone can easily cook rice with a rice cooker bought at an electronics store.

Vegetables (*yasai*)

You'll find that many common vegetables such as cucumbers and eggplants are slightly different tasting or shaped than those you are accustomed to. If you're interested in Japanese vegetables, try *daikon* radish, burdock roots (*gobō*), or various kinds of mushrooms. Organic vegetables are not common, but they can be found at large grocery stores and health food stores.

Fruits (*kudamono*)

A wide variety's available and they're absolutely delicious, but expect high prices. Don't miss the big sweet Fuji apples and the round Japanese pears called *nashi*. Watermelons are reasonably priced in the summer and most of them taste great. In winter, you can enjoy many kinds of citrus fruit.

Meat (*niku*)

In recent years, prices have dropped and variety increased. You'll seldom be disappointed with the quality. Meat counters have a variety of cuts, but the butcher is usually happy to take requests.

Dairy products (*nyūseihin*)

Again, great quality, variety and relatively high prices. Choose from several varieties of milk, cheese and yogurt. Portions may be smaller and prices larger than you'd hope for.

Noodles (*men*)

Japanese love spaghetti, so most grocery stores have a good stock of pasta and sauces. You also might want to try Japanese style noodles such as *soba* and *udon*. Both can be prepared in a few minutes.

Bread (*pan*)

For breakfast, you can find white bread, rolls and French bread in any grocery store. And for dark breads, you'll have to go to bakery shops or the food sections of department stores. But the variety of sweet breads and breads with fillings is incredible. Along with your basic donut, there are dozens with imaginative fillings and coverings — curried bread, sausage bread, sweet bean bread, and more.

Seasonings (*chōmiryō*)

You usually won't have any problem finding the basics in addition to some you may not be familiar with. Soy sauce (shoyu) is the most common. *Mirin* is sweet sake used in cooking. Sesame seed oil is another often-used flavoring. Olive oil and vinegar are also common.

Delicatessens (*osōzai*)

Most large grocery stores have a variety of ready-to-eat foods, but you'll also find many different delicatessens in most department stores.

Desserts (*amai mono*)

Dessert is not a part of the traditional Japanese meal, and so it's generally considered something you buy instead of making yourself. The confectioneries will give you plenty of choice. Traditional Japanese sweets, frequently made with glutinous rice and beans, have yet to become international favorites, but they are works of art.

G o o d *to* k n o w ·

Here are some of the words that you may find on signs in a grocery store in Japan.

- ●酒 [*sake*] ▷ alcoholic beverages (Japanese sake is called *osake* or *nihonshu*)
- ●調味料 [*chōmiryō*] ▷ seasonings
- ●牛乳 [*gyūnyū*] ▷ milk
- ●パン [*pan*] ▷ bread
- ●肉 [*niku*] ▷ meat
- ●魚 [*sakana*] ▷ fish
- ●卵 [*tamago*] ▷ egg
- ●米 [*kome*] ▷ rice
- ●醤油 [*shōyu*] ▷ soy sauce

Simple Japanese Dishes

Cooking up something good

Like almost everything else, the Japanese have taken food from around the world and made it better by making it more Japanese. Examples of typical Japanese food that originated outside of Japan include *tempura*, *gyōza* and *rāmen*. But perhaps the non-native dish that has made the deepest inroads into the Japanese heart is curry.

Curry and rice

Curry roux is available at any grocery store. The basic recipe is sauté the meat and vegetables, boil in water, and add the curry roux (break off chunks of almost any size) and add them until you get a paste (to any thickness you want).

1. Add one or two tablespoons of oil to a saucepan and sauté sliced onions until brown. 2. Cook bite-size pieces of meat or fish and carrots in a separate pan and then add to the onions. 3. Add sufficient water for the number of people serving, put in a bay leaf, and simmer to make a soup stock. 4. Add chunks of potatoes and carrots and continue simmering until the vegetables are tender. Then add the curry roux. 5. Try adding almost any vegetable, a can of tuna fish, milk, a diced apple or pineapple, or even chocolate. 6. Scoop over steamed rice and serve.

Shabu-shabu

One of the first appliances you'll want to buy is a portable range, which allows everyone to sits around a communal pot and eat the food as it cooks. This style accommodates a variety of Japanese dishes, including *shabu-shabu*.

1. Make the broth by adding a few slices of *kombu* kelp — soup bullion will

suffice—to cold water and then bring the water to a gentle boil on the portable range. 2. Remove the *kombu* and get out your chopsticks. 3. Hold the slices of beef or pork in your chopsticks and swish (*shabu-shabu* means swish) the meat back and forth a few times in the soup until it changes color. 4. Dip the meat in a sauce (2 parts soy sauce and 1 part lemon juice) and devour. Along with beef, you may want to try some *shiitake* mushrooms, Chinese cabbage and chrysanthemum leaves.

Simple *nikujaga*

Nikujaga, a typical Japanese home-made dish that's something like stew, consists of beef chunks (200 grams), potatoes (6), onions (1 and 1/2), water (2 cups), sugar (5 tbsp.) soy sauce (10 tbsp.), and sake (2 tbsp.).

1. Slice potatoes, onions, and beef into bit-size pieces. 2. Stir-fry the beef in vegetable oil and then add the onions and potatoes. 3. Add two cups of water and half the seasonings. 4. When the water starts to boil, turn down the heat and add the rest of the seasonings. Simmer for at

least 30 minutes and serve. Try adding any vegetable or meat left over in your refrigerator for variety.

Agedashi-dōfu

Agedashi-dōfu, or fried tofu, is made with a firm type of tofu called *momen-dōfu*, minced green onion, powdered red pepper mixed in a teaspoon of grated Japanese radish, and a teaspoon of corn-starch.

1. Cut the tofu block into four pieces and drain well. 2. Dredge the pieces in cornstarch and deep fry them until golden brown on all sides. 3. Place the tofu on a plate and top with green onion, red pepper and radish, and a warm sauce made with 3/4 cups unsalted soup stock, 4 teaspoons of *mirin* (sweet sake), and 1/2 teaspoon of soy sauce.

Enjoying Dinner

Eating out

For those looking for a nice atmosphere and delicious food, you'll have no shortage of choices in the cities. In addition to Japanese dishes, you'll probably be able to find a restaurant that specializes in food from your own country. An important part of dining out in Japan is to know the basic manners.

Non-Japanese restaurants

It's not too much to say that Tokyo offers almost every type of cuisine in the world. The selection includes Korean, Chinese, and other Asian restaurants, along with Italian, French, and other European foods, as well as American and African restaurants. Some such eating establishments offer the same atmosphere and tastes of the original country, while others have been embellished for the Japanese tongue. Some say that non-Japanese food tastes better in Japan than anywhere else in the world.

Prices vary, but for 2,000 yen, you should be able to find something quite delicious to eat. Expect to pay 5,000 yen or more for a meal with courses. Most

establishments will have menus or even wax models at the entrance to help you stay within your budget. At uptown hotels and the classier parts of major cities, you'll find food and service equal with the best in Europe and the United States, but expect to pay for it.

Japanese restaurants

You may find the food a little pricey, but you'll seldom be disappointed with the taste. Most Japanese-style restaurants will focus in one particular type of food such as eel, *sukiyaki*, *shabu-shabu*, pork cutlets, *soba* and *udon*, sushi, or *kaiseki-ryōri*. They usually also offer a nice atmosphere in which to enjoy your meal. Flavoring is sometimes divided into the

Kanto (eastern Japan) type and the Kansai (western Japan) type, the former being more salty and colorful.

When eating at a sushi restaurant, you usually sit at a bar and order individual dishes one by one. The price per plate at such places are sometimes decided by the shop master on the spot, and so it may be best to go with a friend on your first visit.

While prices may be more than what you're used to, don't forget that tipping is not a Japanese custom — and the service is still great.

Dining manners

—Don't clench your chopsticks in a fist.
—It is rude to tap your chopsticks on your rice bowl to get your server's attention. Say *Sumimasen* loudly instead.
—Never stab chopsticks into the food to pick it up — especially into rice. Most Japanese food is designed to be held between chopsticks.
—When not using the chopsticks, place them in front of you. Sometimes there will be a little object there to keep the tips off the table.
—Don't use your chopsticks to point and avoid moving them around too much.
—If you want to separate a piece of food into two pieces with chopsticks, do it step by step and try to do it with the chopstick in one hand — easier said than done.
—Most little bowls of soup and no-handle teacups are to be picked up and held in one hand and supported with the other.
—Making slurping noises while drinking soup, green tea, or noodles is not rude — but it's not rude to not slurp.
—Don't put soy sauce on your rice.

G o o d *to* **k n o w** . . . .

●いただきます。［*Itadakimasu.*］

▷I humbly partake. (A rough translation of the word said before eating.)≒Bon appétit.

●おいしかった。［*Oishikatta.*］

▷That was delicious.

●おなかがいっぱい。［*Onaka ga ippai.*］

▷I'm full.

●おかわりください。［*Okawari kudasai.*］

▷May I have another serving?

●ごちそうさま。［*Gochisōsama.*］

▷That was a banquet. (Said after everything is eaten.) = Thank you. I enjoyed the meal.

Out for a Drink

Finding a watering hole

If you love to drink, Japan is the place to be. Alcohol has found its way into almost every aspect of life, including religion, business and celebrations. Males make up a vast majority of the clientele at most drinking establishments, but women are catching up in terms of alcohol consumption. And if you doubt that Japanese aren't big drinkers, take a ride on the last trains of the day.

What to drink

Beer or *bīru* has become as much a part of the culture as it is in European countries. Although people are gravitating from whisky and hard liquor to beer and other low-alcohol drinks, there are not many light beers available. Wine is also popular, as is Japanese sake, called *nihonshu*. Sake, with an alcohol content of between 10 and 20 percent, is slightly weaker than wine. It's produced throughout the country in a variety of ways and drank either cold or heated.

The typical Japanese cocktail is called *chūhai*, usually a mixture of about 20 to 40 percent *shōchū* spirits and lemon or grapefruit juice, oolong tea, or hot water with *umeboshi*.

Where to drink

Many people will have a drink at home during eating supper called *banshaku*, but many more will stop at a bar on their way home for a drink. Most restaurants also serve beer, wine or other alcoholic drinks. The most popular drinking spot with food is *izakaya* and for those who only drink there are bars, clubs and so on.

Izakaya: These are drinking establishments that offer great food, a very Japanese atmosphere and reasonable prices. *Yakitori*, little pieces of grilled chicken on a stick, or other foods especially suited for drinks, are commonly served at *izakaya*. Many *izakaya* are crowded with businessmen relaxing on their way home from work, but quieter *izakaya* are becoming more popular, especially with women.

Bars: Bars in Japan are considered drinking establishments with — you guessed it — a bar. Prices and atmospheres vary, so it may not be wise to just walk in off the street without some investigation. You'll find a large selection of wine bars, jazz bars, and other Western-like places where you can enjoy the atmosphere, music — sometimes live — and drinks, but don't go if you're hungry.

Clubs: *Kurabu*, probably derived from cabaret club, is for men who like to have the attention of hostesses, women who pour their drinks and make conversation. Often business clients are entertained at such clubs.

Some drinking dos and don'ts

Being invited out for a drink is a sign that the other party wants to establish a better relationship. For Japanese, getting drunk is seen as a way to establish trust and to let tension dissipate. In a country where people measure every word for how it may affect others, it's no wonder that they need to drink to relax.

Perhaps the first rule of drinking etiquette in Japan is don't pour your own. Let others do it for you and in turn, pour for them. The idea is to keep each other's glasses filled, which creates a sense of cooperation and harmony. Before taking the first sip, don't forget to raise your glass and say *kampai*, which means cheers.

Embarrassing questions

Drinking is the time for being asked embarrassing questions about personal matters. "How much do you make?" "Do you like Japanese girls?" "Do you cheat on your wife?" You can answer and hope everyone is too drunk to remember what you said or artfully turn the question into a joke to avoid answering directly. Such questions are usually attempts to open communication and not necessarily to pry.

[日本の買い物事情] *nihon no kaimono jijō*

How to Shop in Japan

Shopping around town

When you walk into stores, you're likely to be bombarded with *"Irasshaimase,"* which means *welcome*. It may surprise you at first, but the clerks are only providing what Japanese customers expect. While Japanese clerks often bow low to you, you don't need to bow in return. You'll not be disappointed with the friendly service, and clerks are always more than happy to help, even if it means directing you to another department or store.

Shopping at stores

Business hours in Japan are usually from 10:00 a.m. to 7:00 or 8:00 p.m. Some stores stay open until 9:00 p.m. This includes drugstores, so it's usually a good idea to have basic medical supplies on hand. Most stores are open the same hours on weekdays and weekends, Sunday being the biggest shopping day of the week. Days off are usually taken on certain weekdays of the month. Convenience stores are usually open 24 hours, 365 days a year in Tokyo and other large cities.

Paying for merchandise in Japan is done mostly by cash, but many stores and restaurants accept credit cards. Still, some larger establishments that you would just assume take plastic don't, so it's a good idea to always carry enough cash. Instead of placing your card or money in the clerk's hand, put it in the little plastic dish most stores will have on the counter. It's where they will place your change, too. And you'll find Japanese clerks very accurate when making change.

Bargaining for better prices is a tricky business in Japan, especially in Tokyo. But you may have better luck in Osaka. You can seldom bargain at department stores, while bargaining at electronic stores can get you some good deals. Generally speaking, the smaller the store, the better your chances of getting a discount. Pushing too hard or bargaining down a price and then deciding not to buy will give you and all other foreigners a bad reputation.

Packaging in Japan is a bit excessive by most standards, although many stores are now trying to be more ecological. Some people carry their own shopping bags so they won't have to use the store's plastic bags. Supermarkets and convenience stores have started placing recycling containers out front for Styrofoam trays and PET bottles.

The biggest sales at most stores are traditionally in July, August, December and January, but now it seems there is some kind of sale every month. Many department stores will also have a bargain floor where you can get discounted merchandise. Most careful Japanese shoppers check the fliers and leaflets in the newspaper for the best deals.

Complaints about quality are usually handled honestly and quickly. Japanese generally don't complain about very much, but complaints are taken seriously. While language may be a problem, if you can somehow explain what the problem is and what response you expect, reasonable requests will be met. The best bet is to take a Japanese-speaking friend with you.

Shopping at home

If you're too busy to go shopping, mail order is an alternative — as is Internet shopping. Shopping from home is popular in Japan, not only for the range of merchandise available, but also because of the prices. You can usually make good use of English web sites. And if you can get around the language barrier, there are many Japanese sites and catalogs with great bargains. You may even want to check out the Japanese auction sites on the Internet.

G o o d *to* k n o w ·····································

- ●これはいくらですか？［*Kore wa ikura desu ka?*］
- ●たかすぎます。［*Takasugimasu.*］
- ●やすくなりますか？［*Yasuku narimasu ka?*］
- ●レジはどこですか？［*Reji wa doko desu ka?*］
- ●カードはつかえますか？［*Kādo wa tsukaemasu ka?*］
- ●おつりです。［*Otsuri desu.*］
- ●まいどありがとうございます。［*Maido arigatō gozaimasu.*］
- ●こわれていました。［*Kowarete imashita.*］

- ▷How much is this?
- ▷It's too expensive.
- ▷Can the price be lowered?
- ▷Where is the cash register?
- ▷Can I use a credit card?
- ▷Here is your change.
- ▷Thank you for coming again.
- ▷It got damaged.

Where to Shop in Japan

Shopper's paradise

Japanese prices can be expensive, but they vary greatly from store to store. You just need to pick stores that offer what you want at prices you are willing to pay. And that will depend on whether you are looking for quality, low prices or the latest trends. Here are some clues on how to become a skilled shopper in Japan.

Quality

Department stores are the Cadillacs of retail outlets with everything from food to electronic products. Some, like Isetan, Mitsukoshi and Takashimaya, present an up-town shopping experience that offers world-class quality for a price. They also have excellent grocery stores and delicatessen shops on the basement floor. Many offer comparatively high prices for quality merchandise. With bookstores, coffee shops and playgrounds for the children, there's enough to do to spend the whole day at the department store.

There are many boutiques in Japan, especially in Tokyo. World-famous brands have opened exclusive shops in Ginza and other classy shopping districts.

More traditional stores with specialty merchandise are found throughout Japan. Anyone who has been in Japan for a while knows some unique shops, but you can find something interesting just by walking down any street. Things to look for include kimono cloth, unusual kitchen utensils, innovative stationery products and elegant art objects.

Cheap and convenient

Neighborhood shopping streets that traditionally served the neighborhood now face tough competition from large supermarkets and convenience stores. But a variety of little shops specializing in tofu, meat, fish, vegetables, dry goods, rice, dairy products and just about everything else, have everything you need. Become a regular and you may be surprised by an occasional discount.

Specialty food shops are never hard to find. Look for unusual rice crackers, beautiful Japanese sweets, and tasty octopus-filled balls called *takoyaki*. You'll also want to experience bakeries, ice cream shops and cake shops.

Convenience stores, open 24-hours, are anywhere and everywhere. They offer food, liquor, stationery, stockings, medicine and more as they compete for customers.

100-yen (*hyakuen*) shops are sometimes called paradise for housewives. Stocked full of items for the kitchen, home, garden, pet and office, you'll want to stop here first for the best bargain. Don't look for price tags — everything is 100 yen. Some even have traditional

Japanese toys and decorative objects that make nice souvenirs.

Vending machines are never far away. While you hear about vending machines selling everything from fresh flowers to underwear, the vast majority vends soda, tea, canned coffee, tea and other drinks.

Duty free shops shouldn't be too hard to find with more than 1,400 locations throughout the country. Merchandise includes pearls, furs, electronic products, watches and much more. Check prices on the Internet before you buy to see if you're really getting a bargain.

Coffee shops are the place to take respite when shopping. While there always seems to be a serious shortage of places to just sit down when you're shopping, there is no shortage of coffee shops. Expect to pay between 200 and 1,000 yen for a cup of coffee — most places do not provide free refills.

G o o d *to* k n o w ·

- ●デパート ［*depāto*］ ▷ department store
- ●スーパー ［*sūpā*］ ▷ supermarket
- ●コンビニ ［*combini*］ ▷ convenience store
- ●じどうはんばいき ［*jidōhambaiki*］ ▷ vending machine
- ●めんぜいてん ［*menzeiten*］ ▷ duty free shop
- ●きっさてん ［*kissaten*］ ▷ coffee shop
- ●ねふだ ［*nefuda*］ ▷ price tag
- ●ブランドひん ［*burando-hin*］ ▷ brand name product
- ●バーゲンセール ［*bāgen sēru*］ ▷ special/bargain sale
- ●とくべつごほうしひん ［*tokubetsu-gohōshihin*］ ▷ special sale item
- ●わりびき ［*waribiki*］ ▷ discount

Shopping Clothes

Finding fashion in Japan

Just keeping up with fashion fads in Japan could be a full-time job. While fashions come and go everywhere in the world, the pace of change in Japan is breathtaking. Especially young Japanese women are known worldwide as "brandies," but they also love inexpensive casual fashions in various textures, colors and designs.

Fashion among the young

Shibuya and Harajuku are the places to see the latest young fashions in Tokyo. Fashion for young Japanese is a means of standing out, but their choices are inevitably based on what they see on TV or the glossy fashion magazines that line bookstore shelves.

Standing out through fashion in Japan means doing what your friends are doing, but in a slightly different way. One way is to use a different cartoon character for your bag, pencil case, hair clips and so forth. Anything considered *kawaii* or cute will usually suffice. Safe bets are Disney characters, Snoopy and Hello Kitty, a white kitten character.

Fashion at work

The vast majority of Japanese are fashionable and sophisticated dressers. Both men and women usually dress well and look very proper.

Businessmen wear their dark suits like military uniforms. And seasonal switch from suits and trench coats, to just suits, to no jackets and long-sleeve shirts, to short-sleeve shirts takes place with the precision of close-order drill.

Women tend to dress very conservatively, but also keep an eye on the sophisticated trends of Paris, New York and other fashion capitals. There are rebels, but the average woman is always dressed very properly and very color coordinated. The streets of Tokyo are crowded during the lunch hour with young office ladies in conservative uniforms supplied by their companies. But after hours, they dress according to the guidance about what's in and what's out that comes from a constant stream of fashion magazines and television shows.

Shopping for clothes

There are several Western brand chain stores in Japan, and finding casual clothes should be relatively easy.

Clothing sizes may be different, so it's a good idea to try things on before buying them. If you're about average in your country, you shouldn't have problems finding something in your size at boutiques featuring overseas brands.

Clothes are frequently divided into S, M, L and LL sizes, something for a 175 cm man being L, and 2L for about 180 cm. See the size charts below. If you're tall in your own country, you may have to look around to find your size. Waist and shoulder widths are another problems, and so always try it on, if you're not sure.

As for shoes, you won't find a lot of women's shoes over 25 cm or men's feet over 27.5 cm. Department and shoe stores in Harajuku, Ginza and other shopping areas have large sizes, and it is possible to get shoes order made. Refer to the table below for shoe, shirt and blouse sizes.

Suits, overcoats & sweaters

Japanese	S	M	L	LL			
American	34	36	38	40	42	44	46
British	34	36	38	40	42	44	46
Continental	44	46	48	50	52	54	56

Collar sizes

Japanese	36	37	38	39	40	41	42
American	14	14.5	15	15.5	16	16.5	17
British	14	14.5	15	15.5	16	16.5	17
Continental	36	37	38	39	40	41	42

Women's clothing

Japanese	9	11	13	15	17	19	21
American	10	12	14	16	18	20	22
British	32	34	36	38	40	42	44
Continental	38	40	42	44	46	48	50

Men's shoes

Japanese	25	26	27	28	29		
American	6	7	8	9	10	11	12
British	5	6	7	8	9	10	11
Continental	39	40	41	42	43	44	45

Women's shoes

Japanese	23	23.5	24	24.5	25	25.5	26
American	6	6.5	7	7.5	8	8.5	9
British	4.5	5	5.5	6	6.5	7	7.5
Continental	36	37	38	38	38	39	40

Special Places to Shop

What to do with your yen

If you're looking for an electronic product or some other specific item, or if you have your sights on bargains or something unusual, then department stores and convenience stores are probably not the best place to go shopping. Here are some unique specialty shops and shopping streets where you may find what you're looking for.

Electronic products and electric appliances (*denkiseihin*): Akihabara on the Yamanote line in Tokyo is known as electronic town, with good reason. Also check out the little Akihabara near Shinjuku Station. Both on the east side and west side, there are several big electronic stores. The electric town in Nippombashi in Osaka is the biggest electronic town in the Kansai district. Another option is to check the Internet for good buys. Some sites such as <http://www.kakaku.com> give daily updates of the cheapest places in Akihabara to buy a number of different products.

Kitchen utensils (*daidokoro yōhin*): Kappa-bashi, east of Ueno Station, is wholesale shopping streets patronized mostly by restaurant owners. But a walk down the main boulevard past all the kitchen-utensil shops will give you a unique insight into Japan, with pots and pans, models of food made of wax or plastic, and packaging — anything and everything to do with cooking.

Japanese souvenirs (*nihontekina miyagemono*): Nakamise-dori leading up to Sensoji Temple in Asakusa is a great place to pick up something to take home. The back streets of Asakusa are probably the most Japanese of all streets in Tokyo.

Fancy goods (*fanshī gudzu*): Harajuku is the place to shop for an endless lineup of cartoon character-based goods such as stationery, costume jewelry, T-shirts, and about anything that teenagers would die for and adults wouldn't be caught dead with.

Sugamo on the Yamanote line is known as the Harajuku for the over-60 crowd, and you might find it even more interesting than Harajuku.

English books (*eigo no hon*): The main sources of English books in Tokyo are the Yaesu Book Center (Tokyo), Kinokuniya (Shunjuku, Shinjuku minami), Jena (Ginza), Maruzen (Nihombashi, Ochanomizu) and Tower Records (Shibuya, Shinjuku). You'll also find a few shops that specialize in English books in Jimbocho, the used-book store capital of Japan.

Antiques (*kottōhin*): Japan has been around for a good many years, so finding something old and beautiful is not that hard. There are occasional antique stores throughout the country. Oriental Bazaar in Harajuku is a great place to stop by. Even if you don't buy, it's a museum experience.

Discount shopping districts (*yasu-uri shōtengai*): They're all over, but none rival Ameyoko (some 300 stores) between Ueno and Okachimachi stations on the Yamanote line. Walking down the main street on a weekend, and especially in the days before New Year's, is like trying to make your way through a jam-packed train. From food to clothing, you name it — they've got it.

Flea markets (*furī māketto*): Since 1990, more and more people have become interested in recycling. Now you'll find flea markets on weekends at parks (like Yoyogi Park) and other public spaces. They can be great places to pick up clothing, household gadgets, antiques, trinkets and everything under the sun — literally speaking.

G o o d *to* k n o w ·······································

- ●でんきや [*denkiya*] ▷ electronics store
- ●くつや [*kutsuya*] ▷ shoe store
- ●ほんや [*hon'ya*] ▷ bookstore
- ●ぶんぼうぐや [*bumbōguya*] ▷ stationery store
- ●かぐや [*kaguya*] ▷ furniture store
- ●さかなや [*sakanaya*] ▷ fish dealer/shop
- ●おかしや [*okashiya*] ▷ confectionery
- ●さかや [*sakaya*] ▷ liquor shop

[電車に乗る] *densha ni noru*

Doing the Trains

Getting around cities

Even if you know almost nothing about Japan, you probably know that Japanese trains are both crowded and efficient. Most of the major cities have networks of train and subway lines that, when converted to maps, have all the intricacy of spider webs. But learn the basics and you'll soon understand why trains are the more convenient to go in Japan.

Q Can I really get anywhere by train?

A Yes, in the central parts of Tokyo, Osaka and Kyoto. Also in Sapporo, Nagoya, Fukuoka and other major cities. But all Japanese cities also have other transportation such as buses and taxis to complement the train systems.

Metro and Toei subways, and Yamanote, Chuo and Keihin-Tohoku JR lines serve central Tokyo. And other private railways will get you to most other parts of Tokyo. The Kansai area has its own network of subway and rail lines to get you around Osaka, Kyoto and other cities.

Q How do I know where I'm going?

A Ask for a free map at any information counter, and then don't leave home without it. A good one includes all the train and subway stations. Make sure you know the name of the station you're headed to and especially where you need to change trains to get there.

Q Where do I get a ticket?

A From the automatic ticket machines outside the wickets. The hard thing is to find your destination and the price on the map above the machines.

Some stations have the information in English. The easy way is to just buy the cheapest ticket, and then use a fare adjustment machine when you get to your destination.

You might also consider getting an *iO-Card* (JR) and a *Passnet* in Tokyo or a *"Surutto Kansai" network card* in Osaka, Kyoto and Kobe. These pre-paid cards allow you to go in and out of the wicket and also to transfer trains without having to buy tickets every time. For long distances, go to one of the major stations where they sell tickets over the counter.

Q Are trains really that crowded?

A Yes, especially during the commuter rush. The morning rush peaks at about 8:00; that's when station workers push people in. And once in, you'll wonder if you can ever get out. More than once, you'll probably get shoved out by the crowd — just push your way back in. So avoid the rush hours, 7:00 and 9:00 in the morning and 5:30 and 8:00 in the evening.

Q What if I'm in a hurry?

A Many lines have local trains (普通 *futsū*), semi-express trains (準急 *junkyū*), express trains (急行 *kyūkō*) and limited express (特急 *tokkyū*) trains. The price is usually the same except for the limited express.

There are also some special trains such as the Shinkansen (新幹線) trains that get you from one part of the country to another at speeds of between 200 and 275 km/h Shinkansen and limited express trains have both reserved and unreserved seats.

Make sure you get on the right train. In a pinch, just say the name of your destination to a station worker and they will tell you what line to take, using sign language if necessary.

Q Are there discount tickets available?

A There are train passes (*teiki-ken*) for periods of one, three, and six months on fixed routes for savings of about 30 percent if you have to travel the same route every day. Other discount tickets are available, but they change frequently and the rules are complicated.

Discount passes can be purchased allowing for four or five days of unlimited travel throughout Japan on JR express and limited express trains. For the subways, you can buy ten commuter tickets (*kaisū-ken*) and get one free, or purchase a one-day pass.

Q Are there any special manners I need to know?

A As a general rule, no drinking, eating or smoking. Most JR platforms have smoking sections. Avoid crossing your legs or stretching out, especially during rush hour. In short, pretend like you're on an elevator. Trains will often have "Priority Seats" or "Courtesy Seats" that are supposed to give priority to the elderly, pregnant and disabled.

Other Means of Transportation

So you don't do trains

Trains are the recommended means of transportation in the cities, but depending on place and time, other means of transportation are sometimes more convenient. Here's the basic information you'll need for using buses, taxis and other transportation.

When in a hurry

Taxis (タクシー *takushī*) are quick, professional, ubiquitous and a little expensive — around 660 yen for the first two kilometers. Due to deregulation, the price you'll pay for a taxi ride will vary slightly depending on the city and taxi company. The biggest problem you'll probably ever face will be sitting in slow city traffic with the meter running when you know you could walk faster.

Take the bus

In most large cities, buses (バス *basu*) are a minor means of transportation, although they can get you to the very few places trains don't go. The elderly seem to make up a majority of bus riders.

Buses play a bigger role in the suburbs and smaller cities, where they often connect train stations. It's always a good idea to know exactly where you're to get off before getting on.

In Tokyo, you pay around 200 yen when you board the bus and you can get off at any stop along its route. In some other cities, you take a ticket with a number on it, and then match the number with a bus fare on a lighted board at the front of the bus. Return the ticket with the appropriate fare when you get off. Bus cards can be purchased at the bus terminal or from the bus driver. You can also get monthly passes (*teiki-ken*).

Going by long-distance bus (*chōkyori basu*) is usually a little less expensive than traveling by train. There are also overnight buses (*shin'ya basu*), so traveling is a cinch if you're the kind that can fall asleep anywhere.

For those quick trips

Although you may not want to arrive at your more important clients on one, bicycles (自転車 *jitensha*) are often the best way to get around the streets of Japan. In Tokyo and most other cities, bicyclists share the sidewalk with pedestrians. Bicycles frequently get stolen, ... so be careful not to go off and leave it for long periods of time.

While the sky's the limit for prices on bicycles, you should be able to find a good if slightly old-fashioned basket-equipped *mama-chari* bicycle for 10,000 yen that will do the job.

When you buy a new bicycle, the shop will usually register it for you. And re-register any used bicycle you buy at your local police box to save a lot of headaches if you get stopped for suspicion of stealing it. If your bicycle isn't where you parked it, there's also a chance that it's been impounded — about 2,000 or 3,000 yen will usually get it back.

Hotrodding it in Japan

It's hard to imagine a more dangerous means of transportation in Japan than a motorcycle (バイク *baiku*) — although it may be the fastest way to get almost anywhere. With a driver's license, you can ride 50 cc motor scooter, but be aware of the 30 km/h speed limit. And with a motorcycle license from your home country, you can also ride a motorcycle.

G o o d *to* k n o w ··

- ●タクシーをひろう [*takushī o hirou*]   ▷ catch a taxi
- ●バスにのる [*basu ni noru*]   ▷ get on a bus
- ●バスをおりる [*basu o oriru*]   ▷ get off a bus
- ●ていりゅうじょ [*teiryūjo*]   ▷ bus stop
- ●じてんしゃにのる [*jitensha ni noru*]   ▷ ride a bicycle
- ●じてんしゃからおりる [*jitensha kara oriru*]   ▷ get off a bicycle
- ●オートバイ・バイク [*ōtobai, baiku*]   ▷ motorcycle

Tokyo's Railway and Subway Network

The fastest route to where you're going

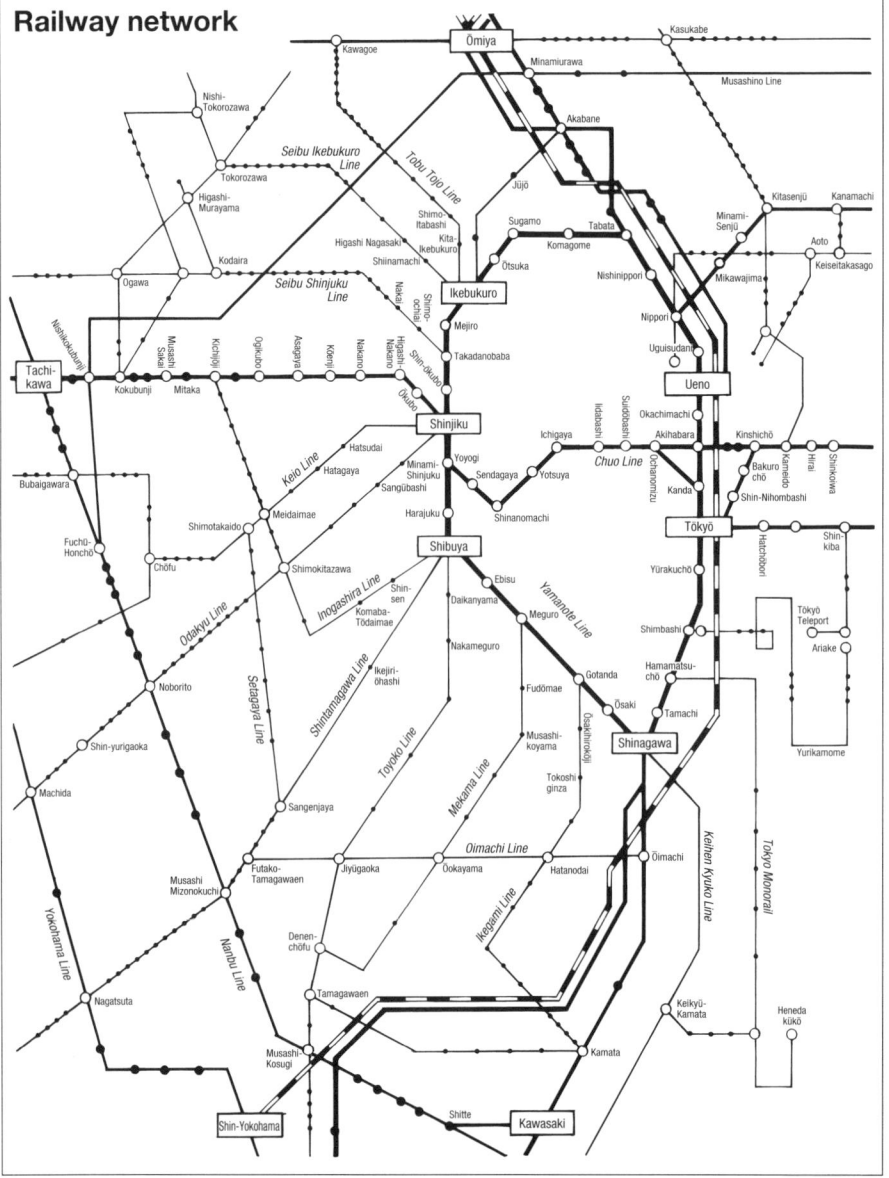

You can get almost anywhere in the Tokyo business area by subway or railway. Subways are especially convenient in the central part, but there are various lines and systems, so make sure you include transfer times in your schedule. Most commuter railway lines connect with the subway lines at least one station.

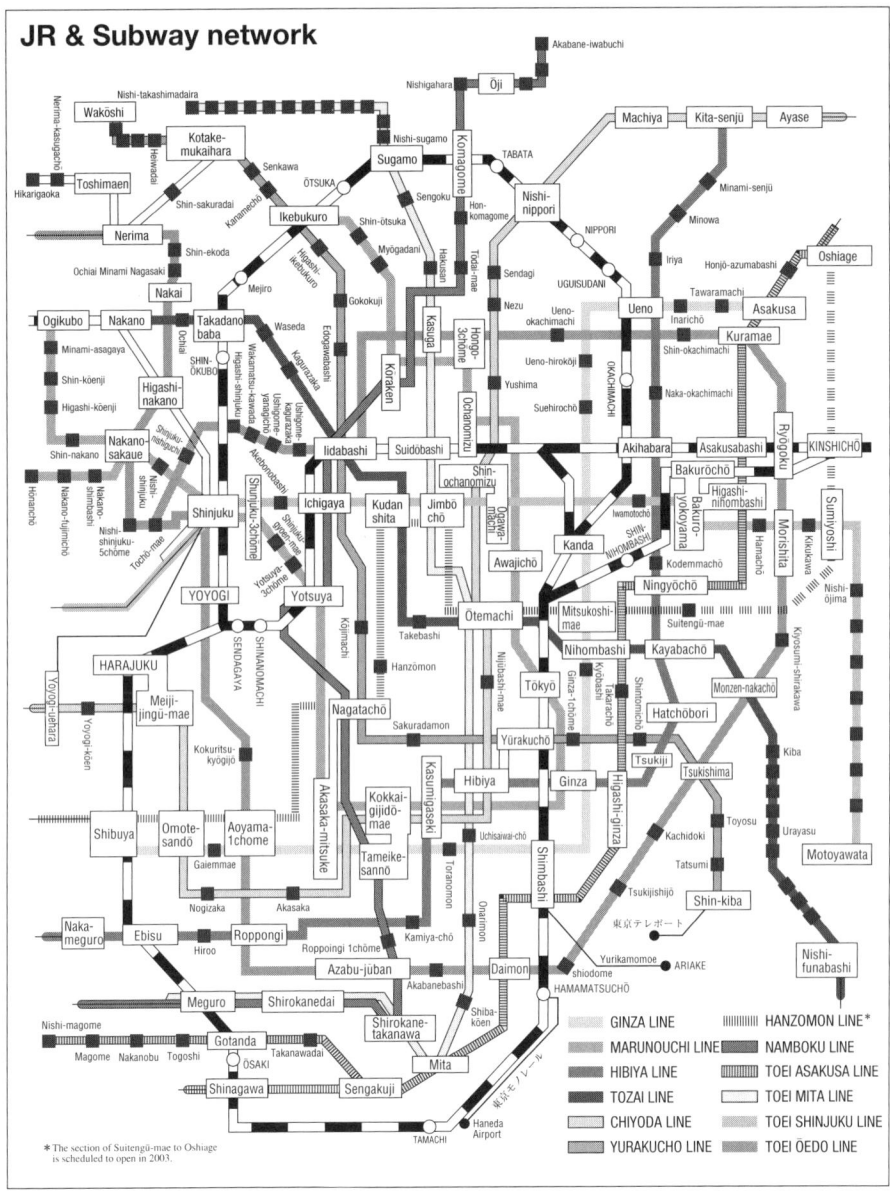

JR & Subway network

GINZA LINE	HANZOMON LINE*
MARUNOUCHI LINE	NAMBOKU LINE
HIBIYA LINE	TOEI ASAKUSA LINE
TOZAI LINE	TOEI MITA LINE
CHIYODA LINE	TOEI SHINJUKU LINE
YURAKUCHO LINE	TOEI ŌEDO LINE

* The section of Suitengū-mae to Oshiage
  is scheduled to open in 2003.

Osaka and Kyoto's Railway and Subway Networks

Learn how to commute smart

Railway network

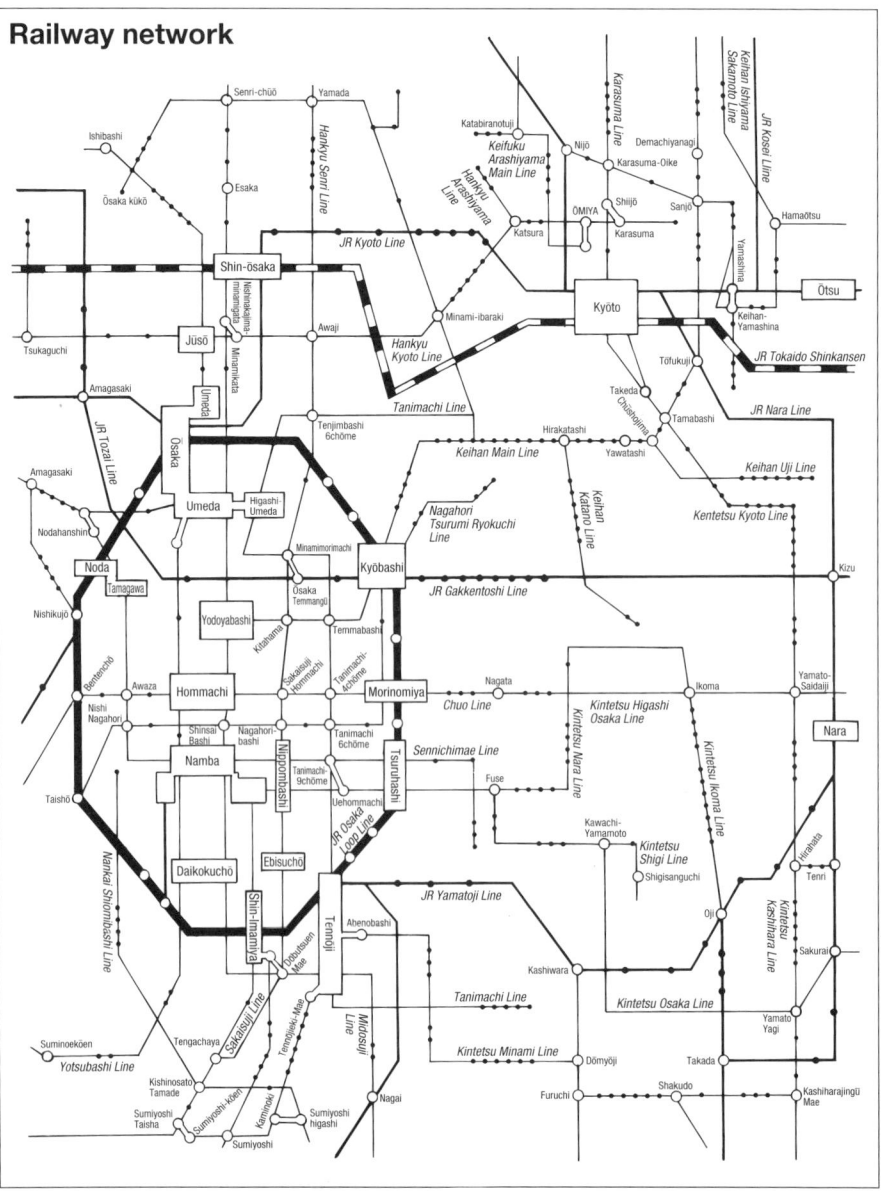

The train systems in Osaka and Kyoto are less complicated than the system in Tokyo. Just remember that Osaka has mostly subway and a JR belt line, while Kyoto is served mostly by subways. The subways and JR train lines intersect at various places, so understanding the system well can save you considerable time.

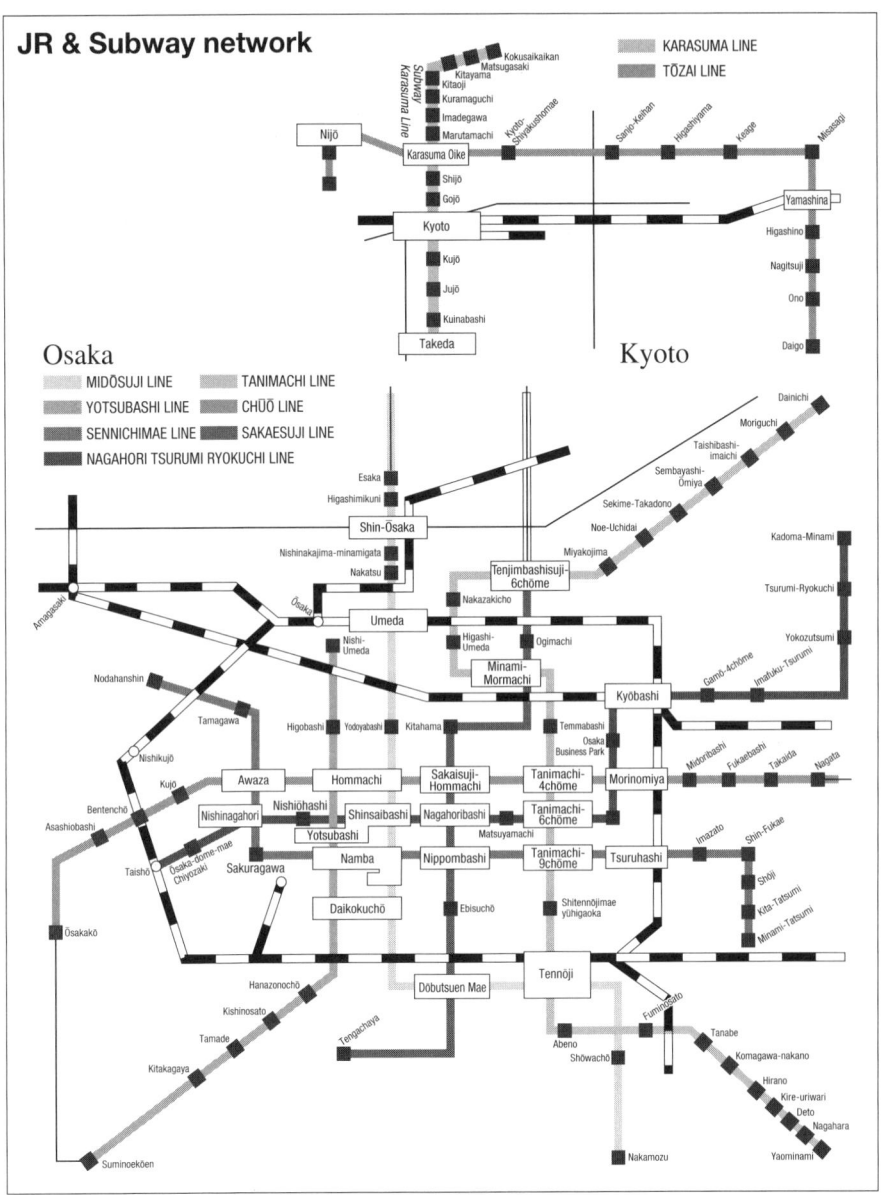

71

Behind the Wheel

Road smart in Japan

More than once I've been offered a car ride because I was in a hurry to get somewhere. Every time I accepted, I regretted it. But if you're not in a hurry and don't mind the crowded narrow roads, traffic jams, and expensive toll gates, driving in Japan can be a pleasant experience.

Japanese driver's license

If you have a valid foreign driver's license from a Geneva Convention country, you can switch to a Japanese license after three months in Japan. Just visit the driver's license center for wherever you live and take the aptitude and driving test. For details check out the JAF, Japan Automobile Federation, homepage <http://www.jaf.or.jp/e/index_e.htm>.

When buying a car

Car dealers are the logical place to buy a car. Japanese compulsory insurance (JCI) is mandatory for every car. Cars must be registered at your local District Land Transportation Bureau, which requires proof of a parking space, along with various other documents. It can be rather complicated, but your dealer will do it for you. There are also taxes — a vehicle purchase tax, consumption tax for purchasing and — vehicle ownership tax. Become a JAF member to take advantage of the various free services they provide.

Rules of the road
—Drive on the left side of the road.
—The driver and front seat passenger must wear seat belts at all times.
—Babies and toddlers must also be fastened into child seats — it's the law.
—There's a zero tolerance driving under the influence policy. Just one drink can get you in trouble.

—Traffic violation penalties are based on a point system, with fines and various penalties kicking in when the points reach certain limits.

The speed limit on expressways is usually 80 km/h. Getting caught going more than 30 km/h over the speed limit on most roads and more than 30 km/h exceeding on highways will result in a 6-point penalty, meaning a suspension of your license.

Road conditions

—National Highways are all numbered and main roads in Japan are named, so it is easy to find where you are going on the map. The latest car navigation systems are also a great help.

—All expressways (*kōsoku-dōro*) in Japan are toll roads — driving from Tokyo to Osaka on one costs about 10,000 yen.

—Interchanges (entrances and exits) on expressways are indicated by signs saying "IC" and junctions are indicated by "JCT." The signs on expressways are green and those on general roads are blue. Signs are in both alphabet and *kanji* characters.

—There is very little legal on-street parking in Japan, so be careful about illegal parking if you don't want to get ticketed or towed away and have to pay a fine.

—If your car gets stalled on the road, contact JAF at 03-5395-0111 in Tokyo, 011-857-8139 in Sapporo, 052-889-5300 in Nagoya, 06-6577-0111 in Osaka, 075-682-0111 in Kyoto, 092-841-5000 in Fukuoka and 098-877-9163 in Okinawa.

—The most common center lines on roads are broken white lines which may be crossed. Solid white lines may be crossed with caution. Yellow center lines may be crossed only when you need to get around obstacles such as double-parked cars. Be aware that center lines aren't completely uniform throughout the country and so play it safe.

Driving manners

Turning your lights on and off a couple of times means that you will let oncoming cars have the right of way. On expressways, drivers will often turn on their hazard lights for a few seconds to warn the driver behind them that traffic congestion looms ahead. A short toot of the horn means thanks to another driver. Horns are seldom used for any other reason. Two blinks of hazard lights tells the driver behind you "thanks," usually when you change lanes.

● ハンドル［*handoru*］　▷ steering wheel
● ガスタンク［*gasu tanku*］　▷ fuel tank
● シートベルト［*shīto beruto*］　▷ seat belt
● フロントガラス［*furonto garasu*］　▷ window shield

Sign Smart on Japanese Roads

Watch for the signs

In Japan, you'll find lots of signs on the roads and streets. For safer driving, familiarize yourself with the important ones, then watch for them carefully. Don't be confused even if the shapes and placing are different from your home country. Here are some explanations that might help make your driving experience slightly less stressful.

Traffic lights

—Red lights (*aka shingō*): All cars must stop — no turning right or left. Many traffic lights have red lights and also green arrows allowing you to go in one direction or another. When the arrow is green you can go in that direction.

—Yellow lights (*kiiro shingō*): Prepare to stop. Do not enter an intersection after the light has turned yellow.

—Green lights (*ao shingō*): You can go but when turning left at an intersection, be careful of pedestrians and bicycles.

Deciphering traffic signs

(1) Stop
(*ichiji teishi*)
After stopping, check right and left. Proceeding with caution.

(2) Speed Limit
(*saikō sokudo*)
If you get caught driving faster than the posted speed limit, you'll find yourself with a fine of 10,000 yen or more. Japan has few sidewalks. Bicycles and cars usually share the same

roads, so even driving within the speed limit can be dangerous.

(3) No Parking
(*chūsha kinshi*)
Any stopping longer than five minutes in the no-parking area is considered illegal parking. Many streets are patrolled, usually by women officers in black-and-white mini cars. But don't expect to get let off easy just because they're women. If you park illegally, you will find that a conspicuous yellow contraption is attached to your door mirror (take it to your local police to pay the fine and have it removed) or that your car has been towed away.

(4) Direction Control
(*shitei hōkōgai shinkō kinshi*)
These signs tell you the directions you're allowed to go in.

(5) One Way
(*ippō tsūkō*)

You'll see lots of these signs especially in residential areas. When you go to somewhere for the first time, you should check the one-way streets on the map beforehand to save having to make extra detours.

(6)Do Not Enter
(*shinnyū kinshi*)
You'll sometimes see several signs on the same street. It pays to be extra careful to determine which one is for your street.

(7) No U-turn
(*yūtān kinshi*)
You can't make U-turns at some intersections. Take care not to make an illegal U-turn.

(8) Do Not Pass
(*oikoshi kinshi*)
Even though it seems safe and traffic is moving at a snail's pace, it's always best to obey the signs.

(9) Yield
(*jokō*)
Don't confuse this with the stop sign. Blue character for yield (徐行) is written in a white triangle. (The stop sign is the same shape but red.)

G o o d *to* k n o w   When doing the trains ·················

<At the Station>

- ●えき ［*eki*］   ▷ train station
- ●かいさつぐち ［*kaisatsuguchi*］   ▷ ticket wicket, gates
- ●ホーム ［*hōmu*］   ▷ platform
- ●いちばんせん ［*ichibansen*］   ▷ line/track No. 1
- ●にばんせん ［*nibansen*］   ▷ line/track No. 2
- ●さんばんせん ［*sambansen*］   ▷ line/track No. 3
- ●いりぐち ［*iriguchi*］   ▷ entrance
- ●でぐち ［*deguchi*］   ▷ exit
- ●ちかてつ ［*chikatetsu*］   ▷ subway
- ●のりかえ ［*norikae*］   ▷ transfer
- ●りょうきん ［*ryōkin*］   ▷ fare
- ●けんばいき ［*kembaiki*］   ▷ ticket machine
- ●えきいん ［*ekiin*］   ▷ station worker/employee

<Useful expressions to buy long distance tickets>

- ●じこくひょう ［*jikokuhyō*］   ▷ timetable
- ●していせき ［*shitei-seki*］   ▷ reserved seat
- ●じゆうせき ［*jiyū-seki*］   ▷ non-reserved seat
- ●グリーンしゃ ［*gurīnsha*］   ▷ Green car (first class)
- ●きんえんせき ［*kin'en-seki*］   ▷ non-smoking seats
- ●きつえんせき ［*kitsuen-seki*］   ▷ smoking seats
- ●まどがわ ［*madogawa*］   ▷ window side
- ●つうろがわ ［*tsūrogawa*］   ▷ aisle side

Holidays in Japan

Sports to Do

Getting the rust out

Sports and exercise can help maintain your health and reduce stress. Lately many people, who are concerned about their health, have joined sports clubs or engage in sports. Many Japanese companies have baseball and soccer teams that you can join, as they are the most popular sports in Japan. Company gym facilities may also be available.

Finding information

The best way to find out how to participate in your favorite sport is to locate someone who is already doing it. Several English-language free papers carry notices by sports groups seeking participants. I checked one free paper and found contact information for groups involved in football, tennis, golf, baseball, basketball, kick boxing, skiing, snowboarding and mountain biking.

Indoor sports

Perhaps the easiest way to get some exercise is to find athletic gyms in your neighborhood or drop by one of the many public athletic facilities called *taiikukan* (体育館). Public athletic facilities usually have a swimming pool and a workout gym with reasonable rates. Many will have instructors and aerobic classes. This is also a good place to get involved in team sports such as volleyball and basketball, both quite popular in Japan.

You're in Japan, so you might want to try marital arts. If making friends with Japanese is a priority, this can be a good place to start. Along with karate and judo, you'll also find *dōjō* that specialize in *aikidō*, *kempō*, kung fu (*kanfū*), and Tai Chi Chuan (*taikyokuken*).

A past bowling boom gave Japan an abundance of bowling alleys. They are usually good places to play billiards and table tennis, too.

Outdoor sports

Tennis courts — even public courts — are crowded and expensive. I gave up tennis when I reserved a court a month ahead, dreamed of it almost every day, and then sat home watching it rain. You'll have much better luck away from major city centers or if you can find a tennis club in your neighborhood to join.

Golf is usually done on the company tab. You'll understand why when you see the membership and green fees. But if you can tag along with someone who has a membership, then an occasional game is probably within your budget. Playing golf gets cheaper the further you get away from the big cities. Japan has some of the best golf courses in the world. Many were designed by the big names in golf, thanks to the unlimited budgets they had during the bubble economy.

Marine sports

Considering Japan's long coastline, you'd think marine sports would be more popular. Japan has traditionally seen the ocean as a place to work and not play, but marine sports are catching on. Sailing, surfing, wind surfing, jet skiing and diving are possible within hours of almost anywhere in Japan. From Tokyo, you'll find the best beaches in Chiba and Kanagawa prefectures.

Fishing is perhaps one of the easier sports to get hooked on. Most fishing is done in the ocean, but there are some great lakes and streams. Fishing for black bass is especially popular.

Winter sports

The Winter Olympics have been held in Japan twice, attesting to the interest in winter sports. Within two hours of Tokyo, you'll find several world-class ski resorts, including those of Nagano prefecture, site of the 1998 Olympic Winter Games. There is even an indoor ski slope near Tokyo for year-round skiing.

Sports to Watch

Enthusiastic fans

If you like baseball, you'll love Japan. There is something about baseball — maybe the teamwork, the clear rules and the camaraderie of the fans — that strikes a chord among Japanese. Tokyo has seven VHF channels and it's not uncommon to find baseball games on two or three of them at the same time. Even at business gatherings, the subject of baseball is likely to come up, so it might be a good business strategy to find a favorite team.

Baseball

Baseball (野球 *yakyū*), imported from the United States in 1873, was once the most common participation and spectator sport in Japan. But now it seems that most people are satisfied just to watch the game.

There are two professional baseball (プロ野球 *puro-yakyū*) leagues in Japan: the Central League and the Pacific League, each with six teams. Baseball stadiums are located around Kanto and Kansai areas with others in Fukuoka, Hiroshima and Nagoya. The league champions meet in the Japan Series every October.

When the All-Japan High School Baseball Championship Tournament is held in the summer at Koshien Stadium, it seems like the entire country tunes in. As it does for the Spring High School Invitational Tournament.

Sumo

Sumo (相撲), considered Japan's national sport, originated in ancient times as a Shinto ceremony, and it remains rich in ritual and tradition. Becoming a sumo wrestler requires more than a big belly and muscles. You have to enter a stable, *sumo-beya* where strict obedience to the *oyakata*, stable master, and your seniors is absolute. Rising up through the ranks, hopefully to the highest level of *Yokozuna*, or grand champion, requires consistent winning, and that means physical and mental strength. Six tournaments, each lasting 15 days, are held every year, three in Tokyo, and one each in Fukuoka, Nagoya and Osaka. All are broadcast live on NHK, but don't pass on a chance to watch one ringside.

Soccer

Soccer (サッカー *sakkā*) is also popular in Japan. The national team is now competitive enough to win in major international events. The professional J-League, with its J-1, J-2, and J-3 divisions, got its start in the early 1990s and has risen in popularity and skill over the years, thanks in part to players from Europe and South America. Japan is producing world-class players and should soon be able to compete with the best in the world.

Marathons

Marathons (マラソン *marason*) are also extremely popular in Japan. The country produces some of the world's best runners and has an active marathon circuit with televised national and local events. Relay marathons called *ekiden* are also popular.

Horseracing

Let's not forget horseracing (競馬 *keiba*). The industry has boosted its popularity in recent years by reaching out to young single women, who seem to have more discretionary income than anyone else.

Sports channels

An increase in television channels, thanks to satellite and cable broadcasts, has added considerable variety for sports fans. Some of the things you'll find on these channels include American football, skateboarding, surfing and skydiving. And you should also be able to find Major League baseball games, world-class soccer matches and professional wrestling.

G o o d *to* k n o w ·····································

● かつ [*katsu*]	▷ win
● まける [*makeru*]	▷ lose
● せんしゅ [*senshu*]	▷ athlete
● しあい [*shiai*]	▷ game, match
● おうえんする [*ōen-suru*]	▷ cheer on
● かんきゃく [*kankyaku*]	▷ spectator
● チーム [*chīmu*]	▷ team
● コーチ [*kōchi*]	▷ coach
● せんしゅけん [*senshuken*]	▷ championship match

81

Theaters

On stage in Japan

The many modern world-class concert halls of Tokyo, Osaka and other major cities provide almost daily shows by renowned local artists as well as performers from around the world of nearly every genre. While you'll have no problem keeping up with the global performing arts scene, you'll also want to get a taste of traditional Japan.

Traditional performing arts

A good place to start is kabuki, an art form with roots dating back to the 16th century. The performances — done entirely by men — include dramatic action, colorful costumes, and exotic dance and music.

You can see it at the Kabukiza Theater near Higashi Ginza Station on the Hibiya and Toei Asakusa subway lines. The program changes monthly, with both matinee and evening performances consisting of three or four plays. Earphones can be rented that give interesting explanations in English about the story, actors, stage and music to help you understand what's going on. The rental fee is 650 yen and deposit is 1,000 yen. Admission ranges from 16,800 yen for a 1st-floor box seat to 2,520 yen for a seat in the back. Prices for special performances in the New Year and summer seasons vary. For reservations, call 03-5565-6000. The Minamiza Theater in Kyoto (reservations: 06-6214-2200) is less expensive.

Foreigners who see Noh for the first time can usually be divided into two types: they love it but once is enough or they love it and can't get enough. Noh, dating back to the 14th century, is mostly a visual experience with elements that include exotic masks, beautiful costumes, slow ritualistic movements and chants.

Around a thousand years ago, two forms of dance called *sarugaku* and *dengaku* appeared. Four hundred years later, Kiyotsugu Kan'ami (1333-1384) and his son combined the two and added a serious Buddhist tone: the result was Noh. The art has been passed down for generations, usually from father to son.

Tickets for both kabuki and Noh can be purchased at the door or from ticket centers such as *Ticket Pia* located throughout the city and through the Internet.

Other performing arts

Along with many renowned Japanese artists, many of the world's great performers come to Japan, bringing opera, orchestras, musicals, ballet, jazz, rock, pop music and much more, so you should be able to keep culturally in touch. Ticket prices generally start at 3,000 yen, but tickets to operas such as those performed in Europe or the United States cost considerably more in Japan they do in Western countries.

Movie theaters showing Hollywood movies, while probably more expensive that what you're used to, are just about everywhere. The only difference is the subtitles at the bottom or side of the screen and the long commercials before the movie begins.

Information about the arts scene is not hard to find in the English newspapers and free papers distributed at shops that sell imported CDs. The English dailies do a good job of covering the local classical music scene, while you can also get annual schedules at the larger performance halls such as Suntory Hall, Casals Hall, and Tokyo Opera City in Tokyo and the Symphony Hall and Izumi Hall in Osaka.

Reservations can usually be made by phone, or you can get tickets at the door or at ticket centers.

G o o d *to* **k n o w** ·····································

- ●オペラ [*opera*] ▷ opera
- ●げき [*geki*] ▷ play
- ●えいがかん [*eiga-kan*] ▷ movie theater
- ●げきじょう [*gekijō*] ▷ theater
- ●おどり [*odori*] ▷ dance
- ●せき [*seki*] ▷ seats
- ●チケット [*chiketto*] ▷ ticket
- ●よやく [*yoyaku*] ▷ reservations

Tokyo Day Trips

Places to go and things to see

Tokyo has many interesting places to see for the tourists, but many business-people are too busy to explore them. Unless you make an effort, you could spend years in Japan yet miss much of what the country has to offer.

Group tour or individual

Most hotels, travel agencies and tourist bureaus can provide you with pamphlets on bus tours and other things to do in Tokyo. One way to get a general overview of Tokyo is to take an English-guided Hato Bus Tours (online or at most hotels). If you think a "fun-filled" vacation means getting lost at least once, then here are some other things you might try around Tokyo.

Traditional tourist spots

The Imperial Palace (Kokyo) grounds, a ten-minute walk from Tokyo Station, is an easy way to go back in time. Tours go by a huge moat, incredible walls, watch-towers and gardens.

Another place to time-slip backwards is the Yasukuni Shrine, which commemorates Japanese who died in war. The military museum includes articles from both samurai and modern times.

A fun and unusual way to see Tokyo is on the Sumida River water bus that runs from Asakusa to Hinode Pier. In about 45 minutes, you'll pass under 12 bridges and get a great view of huge barges, old riverside homes, and Tokyo Tower. Some of the Hato Bus Tours includes the water bus trip.

For a quick but comprehensive history lesson on Tokyo, visit the Edo-Tokyo Museum (Edo Tokyo Hakubutsukan). In addition to the exhibits, see models of 17th century Tokyo (then known as

Edo), replicas of a kabuki theater from those times, a feudal lord's estate, the Shogun's palace, and more.

Ueno Zoo (Ueno Dobutsuen) is not huge by most standards, but it is a pleasant stroll. Don't forget to walk around Ueno Park (Ueno Koen) and see the gardens, Shinobazu Pond, temples, museums and art galleries.

Modern aspects of Tokyo

Tokyo Metropolitan Government Building (Tocho) in Shinjuku is certainly one of the more spectacular buildings in Japan. Ride up to the observatory floor on the 45th floor of the 48-floor twin tower building for a great view of Tokyo.

Walk around Harajuku to see the most unusual fashions in Japan. Nearby is Yoyogi Park with its beautiful gardens, tree-covered grounds and bird sanctuary. On weekends you'll see young girls in psychedelic makeup and flamboyant outfits gathering in the park. The famous Meiji Shrine (Meiji Jingu), surrounded by giant cedars, is in the same area.

Waterfront

Take a walk across magnificent Rainbow Bridge that spans Tokyo Bay from Shibaura-Futo Station on the Yurikamome Line. You'll get a spectacular view of much of the city.

Odaiba is on a reclaimed land on the eastern side of Rainbow Bridge. The newly built area offers museums, concerts, shopping, a huge Ferris wheel and a beach. The boardwalk is as enjoyable in the evening as in the day. You can get there by walking across the bridge, taking the water bus from Hinode Pier near Hamamatsucho Station, or on the Yurikamome Line that leaves from Shimbashi.

You can take a tour through the world's largest fish market in Tsukiji, but it starts at 5:15 a.m. Then, stop by the Tsukiji Fish Information Center and Museum to find out more about what you saw.

Tourist information

Here are some websites that provide tourist information for foreigners in both Japanese and English.

●Japan National Tourist Organization
http://www.jnto.go.jp/
●Tokyo Convention & Visitors Bureau (TCVB)
http://www.tcvb.or.jp

●Kansai International Public Relations Promotion Office (KIPPO)
http://www.kippo.or.jp
●Hato Bus
http://www.hatobus.co.jp/english/index.html
●Edo-Tokyo Museum
http://www.edo-tokyo-museum.or.jp/index.htm

Weekend Trips

Making a getaway

Much of Japan's population is concentrated in the cities, leaving a considerable amount of untouched nature and spots of great historical importance. While there are many things to do within the major cities, there is also much to do and see within a short drive or train ride away.

Beaches and mountains — from Tokyo

Hakone (Kanagawa prefecture): Some of the most famous hot springs in the Kanto district, quaint villages, the Hakone Open-Air Museum, a wonderful museum with a great Picasso collection, and several scenic trolley rides — all within a little over an hour on the Odakyu Line's "Romance Car" out of Shinjuku in Tokyo.

Izu Peninsula (Shizuoka prefecture): Take the Odoriko Super Express from Shinjuku, Tokyo or Ikebukuro about 3-hour to Izukyu Shimoda, and then take a local train or buses to find beaches, or wonderful hot springs overlooking the ocean.

Shimoda, at the tip of Izu Peninsula, is well-known as the residence of Townsend Harris, the first U.S. consul to visit Japan.

Atami, whose name literally translates as "Hot Sea," is a traditional hot-springs resort. The Oyu Geyser in front of Atami station is famous.

Mt. Fuji (Shizuoka and Yamanashi prefectures): The tallest mountain in the country, Mt. Fuji or Fuji-san is the symbol for Japan like the Statue of Liberty is the symbol for the United States. It's beautiful to look at and tough to climb — but worth the view.

Summer getaways

Karuizawa (Gumma and Nagano prefectures), about an hour out of Tokyo on the Shinkansen, has a reputation as being the ideal vacation home and resort area for escaping the heat of Tokyo.

Kujukurihama (Chiba prefecture) on the Boso Peninsula near Narita Airport is also a well-known summer resort. It has a very long beach that extends some 60 km.

While it is possible to get to these two areas by train and bus, a car will let you explore the back roads at your own speed.

History and nature — from Tokyo

Kamakura (Kanagawa prefecture): Only about an hour south of Tokyo, Kamakura is a good candidate for a day trip, but a weekend does it more justice. It was the seat of the Bakufu government from the 12th to 14th centuries, so you'll find beautiful and solemn temples, the giant statue of Buddha, and many historical sites. You may also want to check out the beach, along with surfing, diving, and other marine sports.

Nikko (Tochigi prefecture): About two hours from Tokyo, Toshogu — one of the most famous Shinto shrines — the original wood carving of the see-no-evil, hear-no-evil, speak-no-evil monkeys, the spectacular Kegon-no-taki waterfall, and lots of monkeys make this a compact way to see Japan at its finest.

History and nature — from Osaka

Kyoto, the cradle for the arts and culture of Japan, served as the capital of the country for a thousand years until Tokyo became the capital in 1868. Spared from the destruction of World War II, Kyoto is famous for its old temples, shrines and homes. A bus network covers the city with buses that run every 7 to 20 minutes. Consider getting a one-day bus and train pass (at bus and train stations).

Nara: This ancient capital — older than Kyoto — is often referred to as the birthplace of Japanese culture. While not as expansive as Kyoto, its delicate mixture of history and beautiful nature — especially the tame deer — is irresistible. The Nara National Museum in Nara Park is a good place to get oriented.

G o o d *to* **k n o w** ··

- ●かんこう [*kankō*]　▷ sightseeing
- ●かんこうあんないじょ [*kankō annaijo*]　▷ tourist information booth
- ●ちず [*chizu*]　▷ map
- ●めいしょ [*meisho*]　▷ famous place
- ●きねんしゃしん [*kinen shashin*]　▷ commemorative photograph
- ●めいさんひん [*meisanhin*]　▷ famous local product
- ●おみやげ [*omiyage*]　▷ souvenir
- ●えはがき [*ehagaki*]　▷ picture postcard

Japanese Inns

Going back in time

Tokyo and some other Japanese cities have become so Westernized that it's quite possible to live there without ever having to understand the culture. But Japan does have an enigmatic ability to move into the future while retaining the past. One such example is the *ryokan* (Japanese inn). Experiencing the Japanese atmosphere and service of a *ryokan* is definitely a memory you'll want to take home with you.

Where is *ryokan*?

Ryokan are located throughout Japan — usually within a short train ride from where you live, and frequently near hot springs, scenic or historical areas. Many *ryokan*, some housed in ancient buildings that look like sets from a samurai movie, have been in business for 10 or more generations. You'll be greeted by kimono-clad staff, traditional *koto* music, and an *ikebana* flower arrangement in your room.

Japanese guest rooms

After checking in, you'll be taken to your room. As you enter the *ryokan*, take off your shoes and put them in the shoe locker. Most rooms will have *tatami* mats on the floor, so feel free to stretch out and relax while being served green tea by your room attendant. Instead of beds, you'll sleep in *futon*, laid out for you in the evening.

Most *ryokan* will provide informal cotton *yukata*. These bathrobe-looking garments serve as pajamas and casual wear for walking around. You'll usually be able to get a bigger one if you need it. They're not for taking home, so ask whether you can buy one if you want.

The slippers are for hard floors — never to be worn on *tatami* or in the bathroom. (Don't make the faux pas of wearing the bathroom slippers anywhere but the bathroom — equivalent to dragging toilet paper behind you!)

Delicious food

Dinner is served on trays at a fixed time, either in your private room or in a separate dining room — the menu is set by the *ryokan* and you have little choice. The traditional Japanese food is healthy, fresh, delicious, seasonal, and in great variety and volume, so you'll want a good appetite.

Spacious bathing

Bathing at a *ryokan* is more than just wholesome hygiene. Most have communal baths that take advantage of hot springs, one for men and another for women. Hot spring bathing is a favorite activity of the Japanese. Make sure you wash well before getting in the tub to sit and soak. Some communal baths will have more than one type, allowing you go tub-hopping from one temperature or scent to another, each offering different health benefits.

Rates

Rates are per person, not per room, and breakfast and dinner are usually included. *Ryokan* inns are crowded during holidays and on weekends, so you'll usually find the service much better, the bath less crowded, and lower rates on weekdays. The three most difficult times to get reservations are the New Year holidays, Golden Week (April 29 to May 5), and the Bon Festival season (a week centering around August 15).

An alternative

A less expensive alternative to *ryokan* is the *minshuku*, the Japanese version of bed-and-breakfast places. They are a little more homey, less luxurious, and may only include one meal, but you'll still get a taste of traditional Japanese life.

A word of caution

Japanese inns are dedicated to meeting the desire of Japanese to go back in time, and so you may feel out of place if you're used to Western hotels. Managing without Japanese at a *ryokan* will also be a little more difficult than at most hotels. The Internet sites below will head you in the direction of inns were that accommodate English-speaking guests.

●Japan Hotel Network
http://www.japanhotel.net/
●Japan Economy Hotels Reservation Service
http://www.inn-info.co.jp/english/home.html
●Yadokari
http://www.yadokari.co.jp/home_E.htm

APPENDIX

Weight

g	kg	ounce	pound
1	0.001	0.035	0.002
1000	1	35.274	2.205
28.35	0.028	1	0.063
453.59	0.454	16	1

Length

cm	m	km	inch	foot	yard	mile
1	0.01	–	0.3937	0.0328	0.0109	–
100	1	0.0001	39.370	3.2808	1.0936	0.0006
100000	1000.0	1	39370	3280.3	1093.6	0.6214
2.5399	0.0254	–	1	0.0833	0.0277	–
30.479	0.3047	–	12.000	1	0.333	–
91.440	0.9144	–	36.000	3.0000	1	–
–	1609.3	1.6093	–	–	–	1

eg. speed limits of the car : 50km = 31.07miles

Square Measures

m	km	square inch	square foot	square yard	hectare	acre
1	–	1550.0	10.764	1.1960	–	–
–	1	–	–	–	100.00	247.11
0.0006	–	1	0.0069	0.0007	–	–
0.0922	–	144.00	1	0.1111	–	–
0.8360	–	1296.0	9.0000	1	–	–
–	0.0100	–	–	–	1	2.4711
–	0.0040	–	–	–	0.4047	1

Centigrade & Fahrenheit

$$F = \frac{9}{5}C + 32°C = \frac{5}{9}(F - 32°)$$

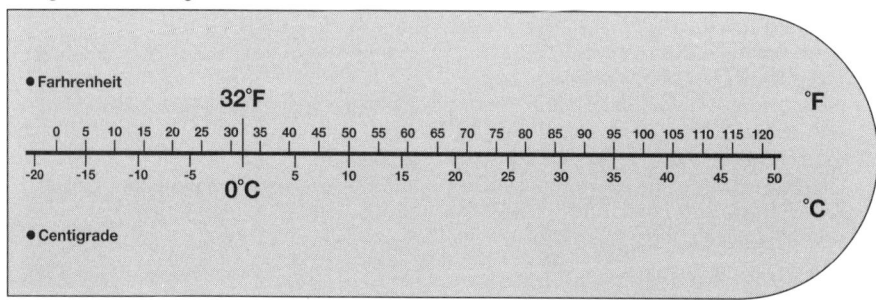

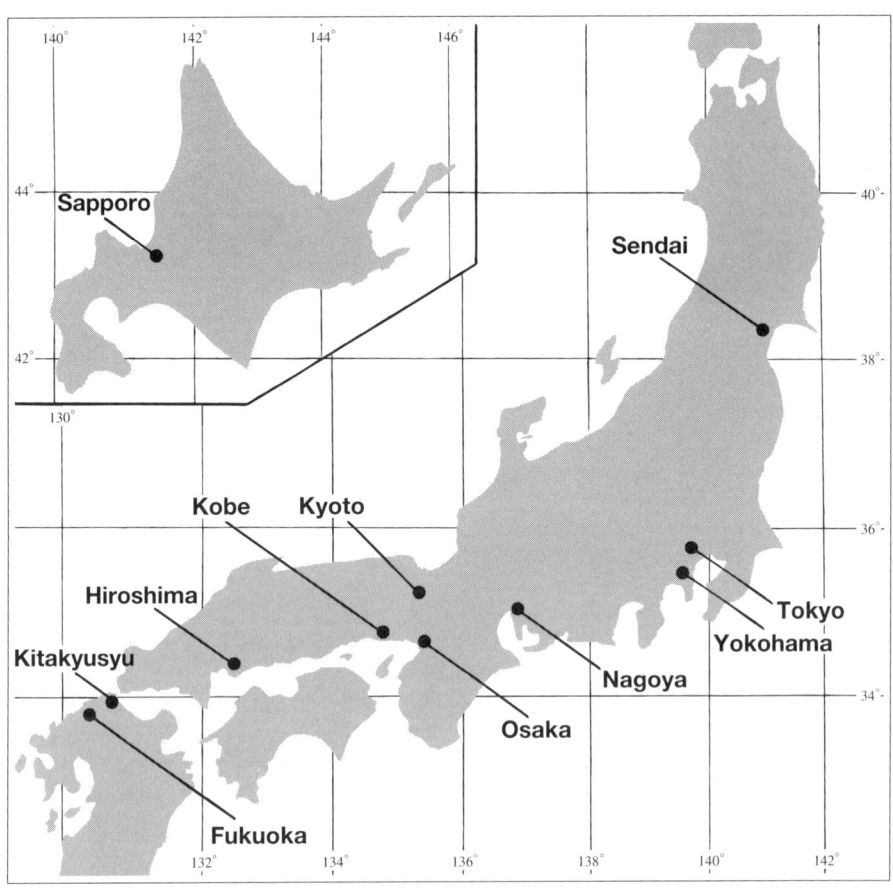

Population of major 12 cities
(Unit : 1,000 persons)

Rank	City	Population
1	Tokyo 23 wards	8,130
2	Yokohama	3,427
3	Osaka	2,599
4	Nagoya	2,171
5	Sapporo	1,822
6	Kobe	1,494

Rank	City	Population
7	Kyoto	1,468
8	Fukuoka	1,341
9	Kawasaki	1,250
10	Hiroshima	1,126
11	Kitakyushu	1,011
12	Sendai	1,008

Source : homepages of each city
October 2000

INDEX

93

95

Andy D. Para

Born in 1959 in Arizona, Andy Para first came to Japan in 1980 with the intentions of staying a year to earn enough money teaching English to pay his way through college. After three years in Japan, he finally returned, and earned a Masters Degree in Social Science from Azusa Pacific University in California. After working five years as a stockbroker and three years as an interpreter, he returned to Japan where he currently works as a writer and translator. He has authored and translated more than 30 books on topics including Japanese culture, English language study, and leadership.